MW00981563

The Collaborator

The great writer, Victor Hugo, once said, "there is one thing stronger than all the armies in the world, and that is an idea whose time has come." *The Collaborator* introduces soccer as a metaphor for global business — an idea whose time has come! Leveraging soccer's worldwide recognition as a game and language, its metaphor offers people, teams, and organizations an innovative and practical model for managing in today's global business world.

The Collaborator is a quick read, taking us on the journey of Toni Burns, a newly promoted global manager. As the story unfolds, Toni is faced with the challenge of moving from an individual contributor role to a manager role. Under the strong leadership of her new supervisor, Ron Posada, she is introduced to a series of operating principles that mirror what happens on the soccer field. When applied, they unlock the "collaboration code" for managing globally.

In *The Collaborator*, Winsor Jenkins shows how soccer's "eleven" operating principles match up with the global business model. Combined with complimentary business competencies, they provide the organizational framework for helping overcome the challenges associated with working globally.

THE COLLABORATOR

Discover Soccer as a Metaphor for Global Business Leadership

WINSOR JENKINS

DW Publishing
P.O. Box 2010
Lake Oswego, OR 97035
DWPublish@aol.com
503-201-0772

Printed in the United States of America

Library of Congress Cataloging-in-Publishing Data is on file.
Jenkins, Winsor
  The collaborator: discover soccer as a metaphor for global business leadership /
  by Winsor Jenkins.
  p. cm.

  ISBN 978-0-9795724-0-1
  1. Global Leadership. 2. Collaboration. 3. Globalization. 4. Organizational
  Development. 5. Management. I. Title

First Edition: August 2007
10 9 8 7 6 5 4 3 2 1

Cover designed: Tina Swanson – YRG www.yrgcommunications.com
Graphic Design: Kelsie Yurk

This book is dedicated to Dee Dee.
As wife and best friend, she is my number
"one" collaborator.

Contents

Introduction

Change continues to come at people at a pace that is both accelerating and overwhelming. This is especially true in the global business world. Competitors sprout up from nowhere. Markets and customers shift at a moment's notice. Jobs continue to get outsourced across boundaries. The battle for talent is unrelenting.

In today's highly competitive global business environment, people are looking for new metaphors and models to understand how change is affecting business, leadership, and employee expectations regarding performance.

The game of soccer is a powerful metaphor for individuals, teams, and organizations competing in the global economy. Taking advantage of soccer's worldwide recognition as a game *and* language, its metaphor offers an operating framework—or model—for helping overcome the challenges associated with working in global business.

The Collaborator lays out eleven operating principles matching up with the global business model. Together, they describe *SOCCER* as a Strategic Operating Collaboration Code *for* Earning Results, *for* Engaging Resources, and *for* Establishing Relationships.

If you agree that collaboration represents a critical business practice for succeeding or *scoring goals* on the global business field, you will find that *The Collaborator* provides an innovative and practical model to help people understand what global business *and* leadership look like—and how employees are expected to perform in the global business economy.

The Promotion

Packing her climbing gear into the backpack and zipping it closed, Toni Burns thought of the meeting she'd had earlier with her supervisor, Ron Posada. They had met to review performance expectations for her new position as manager of international business development for Trans-Global Industries. Often referred to as "TAG" Industries, it was a leading provider of engineered products and services to countries around the world. Its products were used in water infrastructure and power plant projects.

In their meeting, Ron had outlined a number of action steps, including training, for Toni to complete in the next twelve months. He also asked her to keep a journal of issues and concerns she encountered along the way.

They agreed to meet every week to review her progress. She smiled as she recalled his parting remark, "Toni, I'm confident we'll make this work for both of us. Enjoy your vacation."

Toni was apprehensive about how she would effectively lead a team of eight people scattered around the world. Dealing with multi-cultural differences—along with managing others —was a completely new set of challenges for her. On top of that, Ron was asking her to learn and apply a new business metaphor for managing her team. He was convinced that this metaphor represented the most appropriate model for managing people and teams in today's global business world. Learning and applying this would be critical to her success, he maintained.

She was honored he thought so highly of her. At the same time, however, she didn't want him to regret his decision.

Toni's husband, Nick, arrived home as Toni carried the luggage into the living room.

"Hey, I was going to help you with that," he said, taking the bag from her.

"But isn't it nice it's already done?"

He laughed and hugged her. "I have been dreaming of this vacation for a long time," declared Nick.

"So have I."

"It'll give us a chance to catch our breath a little before tackling all the world's challenges."

"You can say that again," Toni said, sighing. "To tell you the truth, I'm having second thoughts about taking on this new job. Ron and I met today to discuss how we're going to make this work. What if I can't live up to his expectations?"

Toni Burns worked for TAG Industries for twelve years. After joining the company, she enrolled at a local college and earned a bachelor's degree in civil engineering while going to school in the evening. She was especially proud of that achievement—and the fact that she was the first female project engineer to work for the company. For the past six years, she had been a highly successful project engineer, working in the company's domestic operations group.

Although her short-term goal was to be a manager, she was feeling a little overwhelmed. She wanted the challenge of managing others, but hadn't expected to start managing on a global level. What did that even look like? She knew her eagerness to learn and strong work ethic would only carry her so far in her new assignment. She had made numerous personal sacrifices to earn her degree and position herself for the opportunity to manage people. Failing in her new job was not an option.

The Champion

Moving up the ranks since graduating from college with a degree in engineering, Ron Posada served as vice president, global business development. TAG Industries gave him every opportunity to take on a series of challenging international assignments. He was well recognized in the company and industry as a solid manager of people. Over the course of twenty years, Ron had moved up the organization because of his ability to manage others effectively to get results. He was a strong believer in coaching and developing his people.

"Why do you think Ron is so confident I can handle the new job?" Toni asked, after loading bags in the car to return home from vacation.

Nick hesitated a moment. He had asked Toni not to bring up

work during vacation and she agreed. He wanted her to enjoy the time off before throwing herself into her new position. Now that their vacation was just about over, her focus was shifting back to her new job. He wished she could have waited until they were back home, but he knew she was anxious about the challenges she would face in the morning.

"I have to believe he recognized your solid performance, strengths, and potential to lead others. You know, I only met him twice. At the retirement party for your former CFO, I overheard a conversation he had with a couple of his peers in the company. He appeared to be a good listener and knew how to ask insightful questions. Based on that I would say he has very strong communication skills. I think you can count on him to be clear about what he expects from you."

"Yeah, he sure is a good communicator," Toni said. "And he is always talking about the importance of setting, prioritizing, and achieving goals! I have never been around someone who works that way."

"Maybe that comes from his athletic background. You know he was an All-American soccer player his senior year of college. Most athletes like Ron are very goal oriented. So are successful business people. I bet he applied the lessons he learned from playing soccer to his business career."

"Good point." She had to agree that everything Nick said regarding Ron's leadership style was right-on. As a manager, he was comfortable around people and always appeared to be accessible to everyone. In the short time Toni had been around him, she was amazed at how much he was able to get done. No wonder he was pegged to replace TAG's president. "But I am not sure you really answered my question. Everything you mentioned is true..."

"Okay, we don't really know. You have to trust that he knows what he is doing. Right?"

"I trust him," Toni said quietly.

"And he must trust you have the ability to do the job!" Nick said.

It was difficult to argue with Nick, Toni thought. He was usually pretty astute about these kinds of things even though he never worked in a corporation. As the owner of Stanwoods, a successful restaurant, Nick frequently found himself in positions where communications skills like listening and questioning were critical to understanding his customers' needs. Without the ability to reduce anxiety and establish trust with his customers, he would be out of business!

For the rest of the morning, Toni did not mention anything more about her new job. However, as they finished eating lunch she said, "Nick, let's stop by the bookstore near my office on the way home. I've been thinking about what you said earlier regarding trust. I was looking at a leadership book recently that talked about effective leaders who build trust. I'd like to pick it up so I have the chance to read it this week."

"You've got it."

"And Nick, I don't disagree with anything you said regarding the issue of trust between Ron and me. I just, well..."

"Not to worry," Nick replied. "I trust that you know what you're doing here!"

Painting Pictures

"Toni, congratulations on your new promotion!" hollered her close friend, Joan, from the company parking lot.

"Thanks, Joan."

"How are things going so far?"

"It's been hectic," Toni said as she approached Joan. "I just got back from vacation on Monday. Right now I'm getting ready to meet with Ron to go over a few things."

"Glad to hear you got some vacation in. The way things are going around here it's hard to find the time to grab a few days, let alone a week. Let's have lunch one of these days so I can hear all about your new job."

"I'll call you next week," Toni said.

"Great. Just let me know where and when."

Toni had used the first two days of the week to catch-up and prepare for her meeting with Ron. Because this was their first meeting since her vacation, she was feeling a little anxious. She wanted everything to go well. Most of all she wanted to give Ron confidence he had made a wise choice in selecting her for the job.

Ron spent Wednesday morning preparing for his meeting with Toni. He had sensed her apprehension about the job, even though he had no doubt she'd been thrilled with the offer. She would be managing for the first time in her career. On top of that, she would be managing a global team, which always created some special challenges. But if she hadn't had the combination of attributes that would make her a good manager and leader, he wouldn't have offered her the position. She had high energy and was well respected as an engineer in the company. Her ability to influence or lead other engineers on various project teams was impressive. He had no doubt she could do the job. He had helped others make a similar transition in the past. And he made it work for himself some years ago!

With Ron targeted to replace the president of TAG Industries in one year, Toni's development was critical to him. His immediate job was to convince Toni that her development plan would help her make the transition from an individual contributor to a manager if she was willing to execute each action item as agreed. Part of his plan was to coach her closely for the first six months. After that, he expected her to be at a development level where he could start delegating many things to her.

Ron was the first senior executive in the company to establish a transition program for people promoted from an individual contributor role to a managerial role. He recognized that in today's lean business world, there were limited developmental opportunities for his people. Many of the positions he had rotated people through in the past to help them gain experience and develop new skills had been eliminated. So it was critical, he believed, to have a formalized transition program in place to help his people. It was his way of ensuring that everything possible was done to develop and position them and the company for success.

The idea of establishing a transition program reminded him of the time he made the transition from high school to college soccer. His college coach had an excellent system for developing both individual players and the team. Once players bought into his system, the rest of his job was much easier to manage. He intended to apply the same strategy.

Toni saw Ron and greeted him with an energetic, "Good afternoon."

"Hi, Toni. Good to see you back from vacation. How was it?"

"Great," Toni said passionately. "Nick and I had a chance to do some serious hiking in the North Cascades for the first time in a while. We saw a lot of wildlife on the trails."

"Nothing that you couldn't handle I assume?" Ron asked as they hurried down the hallway to his office.

"Let's just say we didn't get too friendly with some big creatures we ran into."

Ron smiled. An avid mountain climber himself, he truly understood her fears of the unknown on the trail. He waited for Toni to get seated when they reached the office and then jumped right in. "I hope you didn't spend your vacation worrying about your new position?"

After catching her breath, Toni said, "Nick asked me not to think about the new job while on vacation, but it was hard not to. I think he sensed I would have a hard time making the separation."

"I can certainly relate. I know for me, it would be difficult to separate the two. Good for Nick for trying."

"In the end he was a good sport about the whole thing."

"That's good," Ron said as he settled in across from Toni. "Okay then, are you ready to talk about how to succeed in your new job?"

"I can't wait to get started."

Ron appreciated her enthusiasm. "Toni, I thought the place to start our conversation today would be to talk about challenges you're going to face in managing and leading your people. I want to try to paint a picture for you on the best way to connect and partner with your team across the globe."

"Perfect."

"As we both know, the globalization of American industry has changed the playing field for individuals and organizations alike. As we continue down this path, people and business firms continue to search for meaning and understanding. For example, what does this all mean in terms of jobs, careers, and business success? Is this something that has crossed your mind in the past?"

"It sure has. Frequently, I have found myself in conversations with coworkers on the impact of outsourcing, for example."

"I'm not surprised. We all recognize that technology is leading this change. When asked how technology has impacted leadership, for example, many of us in business continue to struggle for answers. Why? I would suggest it's due, in part, to the dated nature of the metaphors and models we have used in the past to help explain the future."

"Like what?"

"Football is one of the favorite metaphors a lot of people have used to describe business and leadership in America."

"I really don't know much about football," Toni admitted.

"Then let me give you a brief overview. In football, most players have highly specialized roles. In fact, each player's role is so specific that they are constantly entering and exiting the game depending on who controls the ball and its position on the field. For example, there are 'offensive' players that enter the game with the purpose of moving the ball down the field to score points. Here you have a quarterback whose job is to call plays, hand the ball off to a running back, throw the ball to a receiver, and run with the ball if needed. Running backs specialize in running with the ball, and receivers specialize in catching passes. There is also an offensive line whose job is to block for the running backs and protect the quarterback when he is passing the ball. Are you with me so far?"

"Yes."

"Okay, let's talk about 'defensive' players who enter the game when the opposing team has the ball. Their job is to prevent the opposing team from scoring. There are defensive line players, for example, who try to tackle the runner or the quarterback. There are defensive backs who cover the receivers and prevent the ball from being caught. And there are linebackers who may tackle the runner, quarterback, or receiver."

"So the game ends up being a competition between the offense and defense?" Toni asked.

"Yes. At the end of the contest, the team with the most points wins."

"And you're suggesting that football has been frequently used to explain how business works?"

"Yes. The game and its metaphor have been a big part of American culture, which has tended to recognize individuals for specific jobs."

"That's really interesting. I've never made that connection, but I admit I know nothing about football."

Pausing for a moment, Ron thought about telling Toni how much he enjoyed football. He was not trying to bash or be critical of football or any other game. He especially enjoyed watching his college team play during the season. However, he believed that football had a limited value as a working metaphor or model in today's global business economy.

"Let me first ask you this. When you think about how business works, what leadership looks like, and how employees are expected to perform—all in the context of a global business—what image or metaphor comes to mind?"

"I'm really not sure," said Toni, grimacing. "I've never thought about it to tell you the truth. I don't recall the subject coming up in school, but then again I majored in engineering, not business or management."

"That's an honest answer. I'm not sure how many people really give it much thought, especially in dealing with all these issues in a global context. Many people just take it for granted. Also:

People tend to take for granted that what works in America is the most appropriate way to deal with people working in Europe, South America, and Asia, for example.

Toni agreed.

"Let me ask you a second key question. Do you agree that everyone on your team should be on the same page when it comes to managing expectations like how business works, what leadership looks like, and how employees are expected to perform?"

"It makes sense to me. I always felt that my old project team struggled somewhat with understanding how everything was supposed to come together, if that's what we're talking about. And we were not working globally!"

Ron smiled again, but did not answer immediately. "I think we're on track here. The experts call this *alignment*. Most of these experts agree that organizations who attain and sustain alignment with their people, processes, systems, structures—and the needs of the customer—have a competitive advantage in their respective markets."

"Well, I like the idea of meeting and exceeding the needs of customers. Nick does too. So if that is what we're after here, that's great! Serving the customer has always been an objective for me here at TAG."

"I believe there is an appropriate metaphor that can be used to help describe how business works, what leadership looks like, and how employees are expected to perform—all under a global context. That metaphor is the game of soccer!"

Before Toni could respond, Ron got up and walked over to the flip chart in the corner of his office, where he had written:

The soccer metaphor provides a

natural opportunity for American industry to

connect with global partners for understanding

leadership and business on a global basis.

After reading this statement Toni waited for Ron to speak. When he didn't, she commented, "I don't really know anything about soccer either."

"That's the real purpose for this conversation," Ron said. "My job is to teach you how a game like soccer can help you and your team be successful in global business. Obviously, I am not going to teach you how to play soccer, unless you would like to learn. I could put you in touch with the right people. I know there are a number of recreational adult soccer leagues in town."

Before replying Toni noted Ron used the word *teach*. The author of her new leadership book had mentioned that great leaders were also inspiring teachers! "Let me sit with that one for a while," she said, grinning.

"I think a short history lesson here would be helpful," Ron said before sitting down.

"Okay."

"Toni, everyone has their own way of relating to business. For example, I mentioned football a few minutes ago. Again, the game of football has been frequently used to explain how business works, what leadership looks like, and how employees are expected to perform. The game and its metaphor have been a big part of American culture, which has tended to recognize and reward individuals for specific jobs."

Toni, now fully engaged, nodded.

"However many people, including me, believe that the current nature of business is rapidly changing as we move into the twenty-first century. In the past, the business structure was made up of individual jobs or positions. As we sit here today and look into the future, the business structure will be more focused on the team and the work needing to be accomplished. This really means placing the focus on results produced when all positions on the team interact. Because the football metaphor is tied to a past structure focused on rewarding the individual for doing a job, it doesn't serve as a 'working' metaphor for global business." He paused to catch his breath. "What are your thoughts on what I've described so far?"

"I know in my last job I was always being asked to do a number of different things to get the job done. That included, for example, juggling many tasks at the same time, interacting more and more with the customer on a variety of issues, making more decisions with limited information, delegating more to others, and working on a variety of project teams. That trend has been going on for some time. It's all part of getting the job done in the company."

"And I think that's why we have been so successful as a company!" Ron said emphatically. "The fact is:

We must all continue to look for ways to add value

and improve the level of our game.

"So it sounds like you recognize and have experienced some part of this transformation," Ron continued. "And that's good."

"I can definitely relate."

"Okay Toni, is it fair to say we agree that the business world is going through a transformation?"

Toni nodded.

"Is it also fair to say that, while the transformation may not be totally understood, we've both seen and experienced various aspects of the transformation taking place in our jobs?"

Again, Toni nodded.

"And, last but certainly not least, is it fair to say that some past metaphors like football, for example, have limited value in the today's global business world?"

"Based on what you told me earlier, I certainly don't see how football works in business today."

"So since you've answered yes to all three questions, then I think we can conclude by saying there is a need for a better metaphor or model here."

They both nodded.

"Good. This gets us back to viewing soccer as an appropriate metaphor. What is so powerful about its application is that it really connects well to global business. There are *eleven* strategic operating principles related to the metaphor that are directly tied to global business."

Handing Toni a piece of paper, Ron said, "These principles are currently working in business, both here and abroad. They provide individuals, teams, and organizations with a framework for helping to overcome the challenges associated with working in global business:

SOCCER'S GLOBAL BUSINESS
OPERATING PRINCIPLES:

1. Focus On Team—Not Position
2. Understand That Everybody Can Play
3. Embrace Diversity
4. Rely On Each Other
5. Promote Both Individual and Team Values
6. Seek Skillful, Adaptable Players
7. Charge The Team To Perform The Work
8. Empower Players To Win
9. Coach Teams To Respond To Changing Conditions On Their Own
10. Develop Partners On The Field
11. Achieve Cross-Cultural Agility

When Toni finished reading the eleven principles, she grinned. "Sounds compelling so far. I'm looking forward to learning more about this at our next meeting."

"Great. Let me leave you with one last thought before we move to the next agenda item on our list for today." Returning to his flip chart, Ron turned the page and pointed out:

Today's highly competitive global business world—where technology is empowering organizations to be more responsive to markets (speed) and empowering employees on the front line (and in the field) to make decisions, to take risks, to manage change, and to deal with the customer—has become more and more like soccer.

Interesting Insights

Toni had been mulling over Ron's comments from last Wednesday's meeting when his administrative assistant, Barbara, popped into her office to tell her Ron had been unexpectedly called down to Sao Paulo over the weekend and would be gone for the entire week. "Ron has asked Grosvenor Thomas to fill in for him at Wednesday's meeting," Barbara said.

Toni shook her head slightly, confused. "Isn't he our manager of business development in Europe?"

"That's him."

"I thought I was meeting with Mr. Thomas next week."

"I think you're right, but you know how quickly things can change around here. Ron will call you to fill you in on the details."

Moments after Barbara left, Toni's phone rang. It was Ron. "Hi Toni. I'm glad I caught you. I assume you got the message from Barbara?"

"I just did! It caught me by surprise."

"Same here," Ron said. "I just wanted to talk with you personally about the change in plans. Grosvenor Thomas will fill in for me this week. He'll arrive tomorrow instead of the following week. It looks like he'll be here in the States for two weeks. I think you'll find what he has to add to your understanding of our new metaphor very helpful."

"I'm eager to meet Grosvenor. I've heard only good things about him."

"Glad to hear that—they're all true. Call me on my cell phone if you need my help on anything, Toni. I'll get back to you as soon as possible. Bye for now."

Toni was delighted Ron had taken the time to call her. It showed he was serious about his commitment to help her succeed. His parting comment to Toni last Wednesday had been, "My job is to build your understanding of how soccer's metaphor can help you connect and partner more effectively with your team across the globe." With Grosvenor coming in a week early, it was obvious Ron was not going to back off on his commitment.

"It's bloody hot out there," Grosvenor muttered in a mild Welsh accent as he walked slowly through Toni's office door on Tuesday afternoon. "I thought Portland was more like the U.K.

when it came to weather!"

He extended his hand. "I'm Grosvenor Thomas by the way. Most people call me Grove. Glad to meet you, Toni Burns."

"You, too," Toni said, jumping up from her chair. "Ron told me you would be here today, but I wasn't sure what time. Glad you made it."

"Got hung up in San Francisco," Grove barked, frowning. "Normal delays as they say. Just came by to say hello."

"Okay. Since it's so late already, why don't we plan to meet tomorrow morning, say ten o'clock? That way, you can get a good night's rest."

"Sounds like the best plan I've heard in the past twenty-four hours. Cheers for now," Grove said as he turned around and headed out the door.

Delegating his coaching assignment to Grove appeared to be a bit of a paradox, Toni thought when she got home that night. After all, he was going to be reporting to her, yet now he was going to coach her on a subject she knew little about. She knew from her leadership book that good leaders effectively delegate, but she was a little uncomfortable with the idea of a subordinate coaching her.

She had looked up his record and found out he was a veteran of TAG Industries. He had served the company in a variety of positions throughout Europe and South Africa. Currently he was working out of the company's office in Cardiff, Wales. He was well respected in the company as a very competent engineer and manager. He, too, was often called on to help mentor newly promoted managers. His team orientation to the business was a big part of his reputation throughout Europe and South Africa. Like Ron, he had an extensive background in soccer.

Toni trusted Ron knew what he was doing. Still, though, it seemed a bit unorthodox to her.

On Tuesday evening, a Seattle-based recruiter, Tom Haas, called Toni. When she hung up after a brief conversation, she turned to Nick.

"Interesting. That was a recruiter."

Nick put the newspaper down. "Oh, yeah? What did he have to say?"

"He's trying to fill a project engineer position for a competitor. He wanted to know if I knew anyone who might be interested. He said the position was based here in Portland."

"That's interesting all right. I'm guessing that's his way of trying to find out if you're interested."

"You're probably right," Toni said. "He must be recruiting for either National Water or AMERK."

"What makes you think that?"

"They're the only two competitors in town."

"Of course. How'd the conversation end?"

"He said he was trying to have the job filled within the next six months and to call him if I came up with anyone who would be interested."

"So are you interested?"

"I don't know. It might be worth pursuing if things look like they aren't going to work out in my new job."

"That's not a bad idea. It's always good to keep your options open these days. Things in business can change overnight."

Sitting down for lunch at Toni's favorite local restaurant, Grove asked, "So how's the new job going? Any big challenges surface so far?"

"Funny you asked. Ron asked me to learn and use his soccer metaphor to help me connect and partner with the team across the globe. Obviously, this includes you. Going in, this concept was totally foreign to me."

"Right!" Grove agreed. "Ron brought me up to speed on what he covered in your first meeting. He asked me to continue that dialogue this week."

They waited while the waiter placed their salads in front of them. Picking up his fork, Grove continued where he'd left off.

"As I recall, he also said all three of us would meet next week to review any concerns on your part and to continue that journey."

"Good. It'll help keep all of us on the same page."

"I don't know if Ron mentioned this, but we've been using this metaphor now for some time under his leadership! So the good news is most of your team is up to speed. His plan is to bring you up to speed as well. It's a case of playing catch-up with you."

"I wasn't really aware of that," Toni said. "That's really good news! I was sitting here thinking that I was going to have to learn something totally new on the one hand—and then have to teach others on the other hand—all on the run. I was a bit nervous if you know what I mean."

Grove laughed. "Rubbish. You'll find you have a good team who will go out of its way to extend themselves for you. That includes the team helping you understand and apply soccer's operating principles. A key for you is to show the team you are willing to extend yourself here, as well. In fact:

Learning and teaching are good examples of how best to extend yourself as a leader.

"I guess I'm not off the hook then," Toni said, moaning.

"Many years ago a leading management consultant from San Diego taught me that the best way to learn something is to teach it. And I have tried to share that with everyone in my travels."

"Good advice."

"Ron has done a splendid job developing our team. You'll

appreciate Ron and the team once you get more time with them."

"I appreciate Ron already. I'm sure any team he's developed will be good as well."

Grove smiled. "Enough of that for now. Let's pick up your discussion with Ron from last week."

"Okay."

"By the way, did you know soccer is called 'football' everywhere except in America?" asked Grove as their waitress served their main course.

"Why's that?"

"I'm not totally clear on the history of the game. I know that soccer was popularized in Great Britain in the 1800s. They promoted organized team sports, like soccer, to help prepare people to work as a team throughout the British Empire. They used the word, football, to describe what you call soccer. It appears that 'football' stuck with people throughout the world."

Another history lesson thought Toni before responding. Grove's style with her was very similar to Ron's. They both were able to effectively communicate, leading with questions to gather information, gain understanding, and teach. They were also interested in sharing information to build her commitment for using soccer's metaphor. Another sign of good leadership, she thought.

"Why do we call it 'soccer' in this country?"

"You know, I don't know," Grove answered with a blank look on his face. "Never really gave it much thought. Maybe American football got established here before soccer? Americans are always trying to be different. Could be as simple as that? I know the Australians call their football game Australian Rules Football to distinguish that game from football—or soccer, as you call it in the States. May have to do some research here."

"You mentioned that Great Britain promoted soccer as a game to help prepare people to work as a team. Any history you can share here?" she asked.

"As you know, the U.K. has always been a very small country. But back then, they were running a very big, worldwide enterprise called the British Empire. Part of their success in managing this network, to use today's vocabulary, was tied to how well people were able to function as a team across that network. For them the bottom line was that:

Soccer taught things like
character,
discipline,
self-sacrifice,
cooperation,
interdependence,
and the like…
all important to team success.

"Here's another difference worth mentioning," Grove

continued. The word *pitch* is used throughout the world to describe where soccer is played. In America you use the word *field*. Not a big deal really, but another difference worth mentioning."

"Great lunch," Toni said, smiling. "Interesting insights you've shared with me on soccer. I'm beginning to understand how Ron's approach can be used in global business. The historical connections that soccer makes to team development is really impressive."

Grabbing a napkin before getting up from the table, Grove scribbled down the following note and handed it to Toni:

The Soccer Gene is imprinted in the world's DNA

"I'm not sure what this means," Toni said, perplexed.

"Outside of America, soccer represents the world's most popular game! It is well recognized as 'the' game and as a metaphor throughout the world. *Soccer is in their genetic code.*"

"Okay. But, what does that mean here in the U.S.?"

"Ron tells me that soccer's popularity in America continues to grow at the recreation, high school, college, and professional levels," Grove explained. "He says this growth has been going on since the 1970s. People in America have been playing the game now for some time. The soccer gene has been *embedded* in America's culture. Now it only needs to be cultivated. It's all about making a business case for promoting its application in American business—and across the global business world. That's exactly what Ron has tried to do in managing his team prior to your promotion."

Toni smiled. "That gets us back to dealing with how business works, what leadership looks like, and how employees are expected to perform in the context of a global business world!"

"Spot-on!" Grove said, his blue eyes twinkling.

Halftime

Toni finished reading her leadership book. Even though it was Friday night and she was tired, she wanted to have read it cover to cover before next week when Ron returned. It was her first book on business leadership, and she learned a great deal about the topic. She was amazed at how many positive leader attributes and behaviors she recognized from the book in both Ron and Grove. She compiled a list of these—labeling them "leader characteristics" and wrote them in her journal before she went to sleep:

LEADER CHARACTERISTICS:

Strong Communicator
Plans Ahead
Inspires
Trustworthy
Accessible
Systems Thinker
Coaches
Focused
Teaches
Positive
Dependable
Builds Commitment
Builds Competence
Effectively Delegates

Nick was already up making coffee when Toni wandered into the kitchen the next morning. "How about I make omelets?"

"You won't hear any arguments from me," Nick said as he poured them both coffee. "You seem to be in good spirits this morning."

"Yeah, it was a pretty good week. Going in, I was a little surprised and disappointed when I found out that Ron was called out of town. But he came through with a good back-up plan."

"You weren't sure you could trust him?"

"Not really. It was myself I was second guessing."

"Hey Nick," shouted Toni from across the backyard. "I forgot to tell you last night that Grove offered to take me to Delta Park this afternoon to watch a soccer game. He said there's a couple of good teams playing today. He wants to see how well they play soccer here in the States. He offered to give me some pointers on the game. Want to come?"

"I need to go into work myself for a bit. But I expect to hear all about it later."

As he ate lunch, Grove thought about today's game. He hoped to use it as an opportunity to coach Toni on Ron's approach to managing the business.

Grove mulled over Ron's decision to promote Toni. So far, he thought it had been a wise choice. She was eager to learn and absorbed information and concepts quickly.

Earlier in his career he would have jumped at the opportunity to take this job. However, his health wasn't what it once was, and he couldn't imagine leaving Wales, so he had declined Ron's offer to take the job. He was glad Ron wanted to promote the use of soccer in the business with Toni. He recalled when he and Ron started down that path some years ago. Ron was obviously a quick study. He had played the game and was able to see soccer's connections to international business, especially after Ron completed a few overseas assignments early in his career.

With Toni, the challenges to bring her up to speed on soccer's application to managing would be different. On the upside, she had a good education and solid experience in project management and had served as a team leader. She was also someone who had a *strong* capacity to quickly learn new behaviors. On the downside she had limited management and international business experience. Plus, her understanding of soccer and its use as an operating framework was totally new. So Ron's coaching skills were really going to be put to the test.

A Match Made In...

The following Wednesday came quickly. Toni had not seen Ron since his return from Brazil, although she had heard he had been in his office on Tuesday. Thinking that her meeting with Ron could be postponed due to his late return on Monday, she called Barb as soon as she got to her office. To her surprise, the meeting was still on his schedule.

"Greetings," Grove said as he stepped into Toni's office. "I saw Ron briefly last night. He looked a little tired, but was his usual cheery self."

"How did things go in Brazil?"

"About as well as can be expected. He had a pretty irate customer to deal with. Something about quality specs changing. The customer claimed he didn't know anything about the change. He threatened to pull the plug on the project, I guess."

"Did Ron get it solved?" Toni asked.

37

"I'm sure he did. My guess, he wouldn't be here if it wasn't resolved. Ron's an excellent problem solver. He usually finds a way to come up with a solution for both the company and the customer."

"Sounds like he's a win-win negotiator," Toni said.

"By the way. I won't be joining you and Ron today. Got my own emergency to deal with back in the U.K. However, I did send an e-mail to Ron last night summarizing our conversation from last week. I'm sure you two will get on without me. I'll see you Friday before I leave. Cheers."

"Thanks Grove. See you Friday."

Ron spent his lunch hour preparing for his meeting with Toni. From the sound of Grove's e-mail, things went well last week. He was a little surprised to learn they went to a soccer game over the weekend. Good work on Grove's part, he thought.

"How did you feel about Grove sitting in for me last week?" Ron asked Toni as they sat down in his office.

"Mixed feelings, initially."

"How so?"

"Well, I struggled with the idea of a direct report coaching me. Sort of a paradox, I guess. But then, I got over it."

Pausing for a moment, Ron got up from his chair and walked over to the window facing the Cascade Mountains to the east.

"Your response is somewhat predictable, Toni," he said. "In fact it's something I anticipated. Most *new* managers struggle with the idea of a direct report coaching them. But in today's world, you can't expect to know or do everything. So while it appears to be a paradox, I encourage this behavior as part of our team charter. We all help or coach each other as needed. In the end, it represents one of many paradoxes you will have to accept and deal with as a manager."

This reminded Toni of Grove's comment last week when he said she would start to appreciate Ron once she got more time with him. This was one of those "moments of appreciation," she thought.

"When we last saw each other, I left you with a thought regarding the global business. I specifically stated that the global business world has become more and more like soccer! Today I would like to really start building your understanding of how that works. You recall from our last meeting that I talked briefly about soccer's operating principles:

SOCCER'S GLOBAL BUSINESS
OPERATING PRINCIPLES:

1. Focus On Team—Not Position

2. Understand That Everybody Can Play

3. Embrace Diversity

4. Rely On Each Other

5. Promote Both Individual and Team Values

6. Seek Skillful, Adaptable Players

7. Charge The Team To Perform The Work

8. Empower Players To Win

9. Coach Teams To Respond To Changing
   Conditions On Their Own

10. Develop Partners On The Field

11. Achieve Cross-Cultural Agility

"Before covering these in detail," Ron said. "Let's talk about what you learned in your meeting with Grove last week."

"He did a great job explaining things. I appreciated all of his insights, especially what he said about Great Britain's promotion of soccer in the 1800s to help build teamwork for managing its global network," Toni said. In fact, she had written in her journal that:

Great Britain's situation presented interesting

parallels to the challenges we are faced with

today in dealing with the global business world!

Ron nodded and leaned forward. "When he first shared that with me, I had the same reaction. It helps to study your history and understand the past to help build your future."

"I was a little surprised to learn that you had been using this metaphor with the team before I got the job," said Toni.

"Hmmm? I guess I forgot to tell you that before I got called away," Ron said. "My apologies. Hopefully you took it as good news. We have been using it for the past four years. It's been a big part of the team's success so far."

"Grove talked about the soccer gene," Toni said. "I had never thought about it quite that way."

"That's why I see this approach to managing our business as a *natural* opportunity for us to connect and partner with our global business teammates. Soccer is regarded by many as the world's sport. It also represents a common language. Why not try and take advantage of the opportunity to *leverage* this in the business—both here and abroad?"

Toni pondered this. It certainly stimulated her thinking about possibilities. She knew he was using the metaphor as a figure of speech to help her and others reach a destination—a *map* to help describe the global business world with all its meanings around how business works, what leadership looks like, and how employees are expected to perform. She was also impressed with his foresightedness. Thinking back to her leadership book, the author had mentioned this as a positive leader attribute or behavior. She would have to add this to her journal, she thought.

"Are you ready then for another short history lesson?" Ron asked.

Toni nodded.

"When we look at how some past metaphors, like American football, came to be recognized in American culture, it's a matter of understanding that their growth coincided with the industrial development in this country. The mind-set of business leaders in the late 1800s through the 1970s frequently called for *command and control* leadership, a highly directive leadership style that was the dominant leadership style throughout the U.S. since its birth as a nation. The style was needed at the time emphasizing characteristics such as dominance, self-preservation, respect for authority, and discipline. During this period organizations were hierarchical. That was the style—and model—applied in the church, military, and business. And football, for example, taught leadership skills consistent with that model."

"And you're obviously suggesting that better metaphors are needed to match up with the new global business model," Toni said.

"Exactly. When we go back in the early 1900s and look at the mass production world of work promoted by Frederick Taylor under the label of 'scientific management,' we find a business model that called for job specialization. Discipline, for example, was a dominant behavior expected on the part of employees. Again, football as a game and its use as a metaphor were a fit for that business model. But we know today's global business model calls for different thinking."

"How business works, what leadership looks like, and how employees are expected to perform," she said, smiling from ear to ear.

"Why not?" Ron said, pressing forward. "We all know the model is global in scale, an *interdependent* network. We know new or different *skills and values* are needed to effectively perform under this *knowledge-intensive* global business environment. We know today's global business world is increasingly *decentralized* and *time-challenged* with the pressure to continually make better decisions to survive."

"But what we don't know—or have," Toni found herself saying again, "are metaphors to help people understand global business. That's where our metaphor comes into play."

"As you will learn in future meetings, the *match* or parallels between the two are striking!"

It's All in the Game

Toni's meeting with Ron last week had gone well. Her commitment to using his metaphor was growing as was her competence for understanding its application in global business.

She felt comfortable with Ron's leadership style. She could see a shift in his communications. When they first met, he did most of the talking and would ask an occasional question. Now, their dialogue was more two-way, with both asking questions of each other to help clarify and gain understanding. All in all she was feeling more positive about her progress and their relationship. In her journal, she added a number of new leader attributes and behaviors she saw in Ron:

LEADER CHARACTERISTICS:

Honest
Sense of Humor
Anticipates
Committed
Problem Solver
Win-Win Negotiator
Admits Mistakes
Motive Arouser
Foresighted

She wondered just how long this list would get.

That Monday afternoon Ron stopped by to let her know he needed to return to Sao Paulo the following week to meet with Ricardo Aurelio, president of Sentra Development Group. He invited her to join him so she would have the opportunity to meet Carlos Rio, manager of business development in South America. Like Grove, he would be on the team reporting to her.

Toni hoped she would be as delighted with Carlos as she had been with Grove. His knowledge of the business was a real asset. She now understood why he had such a strong reputation when it came to mentoring and team building.

Ron's day progressed with a few surprises. His return to Brazil next week to meet with an upset customer was unexpected. However, he knew the value of being decisive when it came to dealing with customer issues, real or imagined. He saw the trip as an opportunity to introduce Toni to Carlos, so all was not lost.

He was very satisfied with Toni's progress to date. Her commitment to learning was high. She was learning quickly in all areas of her new job, including gaining competence in soccer's application to the business. His job was to keep developing her commitment and competence. That way she would move forward rather than regress as she learned the new job. Regression in a new job was something he anticipated with any employee, including Toni. A big part of his success, he believed, was tied to how well he was able to help her work through this, if needed.

"Toni, this is Tom Haas. How are you this afternoon?"

"Fine, thanks"

"Glad to hear it. Toni, I am going to be in Portland tomorrow. I was wondering if I could talk you into having a cup of coffee with me in the morning, say seven o'clock at the Coffee Club on Jefferson and Third? I think that's close to your office."

Before responding Toni thought about the idea of "keeping her options open" in today's business world. "Okay. But I only have about thirty minutes."

"That will work."

Tuesday morning Toni walked into the Coffee Club, surprised

to find it empty. After ordering a latte, she turned to see a man enter the shop.

"Are you Toni Burns by any chance?" he asked.

"Yes I am."

"I'm Tom Haas," he said while shaking hands. "Thanks so much for taking time out of your busy schedule to meet with me."

"Today is just one of those days when I need to be in the office," Toni said, grinning nervously, as they sat at a table in the corner of the coffee shop.

"I understand. Since we only have a few minutes, let me get to the point. My firm has targeted you for the position we talked about earlier. That's why I wanted to meet you."

"Why me?"

"Let me give you the short answer. Through our industry research and contacts, we have been told that you are an excellent project engineer. As I may have said earlier, good engineers are hard to find, especially in your industry."

"I've heard that before," she said, wincing slightly.

"May I ask what your current role is?"

"I was recently promoted to the position of manager of global business development."

"And before that you were a project engineer?"

"Yes. For the previous six years."

"That must mean you work for Ron Posada?"

"Yes."

"Good man. He's big on all that 'team stuff' from what I hear."

"The whole company is," Toni replied with a confident tone in her voice.

"Well, the firm I represent is more traditional in how they manage, if you know what I mean. I can't tell you who I represent at this time."

"I understand."

"Toni, I would like to leave you with an information packet: job description, pay grade and range and key benefits. As I said before, we have some time here. If you're interested in pursuing this opportunity, please call me. At that point, I would meet with you again and fill you in on the company. From there we would schedule you to meet with the hiring manager. If you decide to pursue this, the process will be handled in a highly confidential manner. Our firm makes that guarantee. Any questions?"

"No. Not really."

"It's been nice meeting with you. Thanks again, and have a great day."

"Thank you," Toni said as she rose to leave.

Ron had suggested in an earlier meeting that Toni meet his father. That way, he thought, she would have the ability to hear a coach's perspective on soccer's inherent benefits to individuals, teams, and organizations.

As Toni and Ron walked across the university campus on Tuesday afternoon to meet Ron's father, Toni felt surprisingly excited. Although Ron only talked about him briefly up to this point in time, she heard others in the office rave about him. He had coached Ron in soccer from the time he was a young boy through high school. He was so effective that Ron earned a scholarship to play soccer at a major university.

"Dad is now retired as a high school coach," Ron said. "For the past few years he has been volunteering as an assistant coach here at the university for the women's team."

"I bet he has a lot to offer the team."

"I've heard he's had a real positive impact. It's also kept him in the game, which is good. Before we meet Dad, let me give you a running start on what he's going to share today by saying:

Soccer is not position-driven

"The team's work consists of advancing the ball to score goals while defending its own goal to keep the opponent from scoring. Eleven players on each team are called upon to play ninety minutes, divided into two, forty-five minute halves. Because soccer is not position-driven, you find players moving up and down the field doing *many* things and serving *various* roles over the course of the game. For example, a player may be playing offense, trying to score a goal at one time. A minute later, that same player may be defending or trying to stop an opponent from advancing the ball down the field."

"Grove pointed that out last Saturday at the game. It was really interesting to see how players changed roles at a moment's notice. It was also very apparent they had to be able to think while playing—and play while thinking—to compete."

"That's why Grove refers to soccer as a 'thinking' persons sport and firmly believes in its application to global business. Again, we ask our people to do the same thing."

"Good point."

"From your experience on Saturday, you know that each team has a goalkeeper. These are the only players who may be described as *partially* position-driven. This means they can use their hands to keep their opponent from scoring a goal. This is only limited, however, to a very small part of the playing field in front of each goal area. The goalkeeper also has the flexibility to move out of that playing area and assist other teammates as needed. Once goalkeepers leave the goal area, however, they can no longer use their hands. This means they are no longer position–driven."

"Your description so far really sounds like the global business model," Toni said. "I can definitely relate to the need to be skillfully adaptable and play various roles in my job."

"Again, think about how your old job was becoming increasingly decentralized and time-challenged. And the future has not changed. In fact, we all must be able to continually make better decisions on the global business field to help the company survive!"

Toni nodded.

"Toni, I'd like you to meet my father," Ron said as they were interrupted by a gentleman walking down the stairs in front of them.

"Nice to meet you, Toni. Please call me Alex. Ron has mentioned you in the past few weeks. I understand you are now on his global business team. Congratulations!"

"Thank you. I've been looking forward to meeting you," Toni said, extending her hand to greet him.

"As you know, Dad was my soccer coach through high school," Ron said with a broad grin on his face. "He taught me everything I know about the game of soccer—and the game of life for that matter."

"Maybe the game of life," Alex said, "but not the game of soccer. You had a pretty good college coach as I remember. Let's give him credit here!"

"Okay. You win on that one," Ron said while taking a seat on the steps. "Toni, I asked Dad to meet with us this afternoon to give you his perspective on soccer. He has a pretty unique perspective to share with you on the game and how it relates to leadership development, for example."

"Thanks for the introduction Ron. Let's hope I can live up to the billing."

"Now, don't be so modest," Ron teased.

"First of all," Alex said, "soccer is a very attractive sport to play, especially for female athletes. When we look at the prerequisites for playing soccer, there really are relatively few, if any! Soccer players come in all shapes and sizes. Unlike a number of other sports where size is typically seen as a prerequisite—and advantage— soccer does not have that built-in limitation. So:

Everybody Can Play

"There's a story I like to share with people to illustrate this point," Alex continued. "Back in 1976 I had the opportunity to meet Pele, the great Brazilian soccer player. This happened in Seattle before the North American Soccer League's championship game. Many people today regard Pele as the greatest soccer player to have played the game—in the world! The one thing that impressed me the most about meeting him was his size. I am 5'10"...I would guess that he was 5'7"...maybe? I had seen him on TV a number of times playing in the world cup games for Brazil, but I had no idea he was that small. So, I like to tell folks that in soccer size does *not* matter!"

"That's a great story!" Toni said. "I bet it really resonates with everyone you share it with."

"Thanks, it's one of my favorites."

"The game of soccer crosses other personal boundaries as well," Ron said. "Besides gender, we're talking about age, race, and ethnic background for example."

"So you find diversity," Alex said, "present in the make-up of players and coaches on many of the great professional teams in Europe and throughout the world. Diversity brings strength to soccer teams and reinforces the *universal* partnership the world has for the game."

More and more, Ron was totally convinced that:

Diversity is a prerequisite for American industry

in partnering and competing in a

global business world.

Ron saw the need to embrace diversity as a key ingredient to competing globally. Here, TAG Industries had to be the "best" player in its respective markets. This translated into being totally customer focused in terms of speed, cost, quality, service, and the like. Ron was convinced the only way he could achieve and sustain this status was through a *team orientation built on collaboration.* And the only way he knew how to achieve this was through embracing diversity, where people accepted individual differences as strengths. Here he was thinking of diversity in its broadest sense: skills, talents, functions, personalities, race, age, gender, cultures, generations, etc. Perhaps most important was the need for diversity of *ideas*. Not only would diversity help to attract the best talent in the world, it would serve as his springboard for establishing team trust. In the end, without team trust there was no way his people would be able and willing to effectively collaborate.

"The women that I help coach here at the university," Alex continued, "view soccer as the *only* game that provides them with the opportunity to gain team skills."

Toni looked puzzled. "Can you clarify that?"

"They would tell you that soccer provides them with a better understanding of the interdependent nature of the team experience. They can't find that same experience playing other sports."

For a moment, Ron was reminded of a mentor who predicted some time ago that the number of women entering the business world and management ranks would continue to grow. At the same time he was promoting soccer as the only *real* team sport that would provide the kind of learning opportunity for women that could be readily transferred from the playing field to the business field. This all had to do with understanding that the successful leader in the future had to have a team orientation, with the *network* representing the future global business model in organizations.

"Mind if I paraphrase what you've said?" Toni asked.

Alex grinned as Toni restated his premise:

Soccer provides the best example of what the *interdependent* **nature of the team experience looks like!**

"No question about it!" Alex said emphatically. "Male or female, it doesn't matter what gender we're talking about. The learning connection here is the same. Ron, you played the game at a pretty high level. Would you agree?"

"Absolutely! When you look at the interdependent nature of the game, you have to recognize that associated leadership skills like collaboration, for example, are learned as a result of playing the game. The fact that a mutual dependency exists between players promotes *collaboration* on the soccer field."

"Grove pointed that out at the game. He went on to say that collaboration may become the number one business practice leading to success. This was based on the ever-increasing economic interdependence taking place in the global economy."

"Grove's definitely right on there," Ron said.

Before responding, Toni was reminded of her history lesson with Grove:

Soccer taught things like character, discipline, self-sacrifice, cooperation, interdependence, and the like... all important to team success.

"Are you suggesting, too," asked Toni, "that people in management positions who have not played a *real* team game like soccer may be at a disadvantage working in global business?"

"To some degree—yes," Ron said. "Again, all one has to do is look at the experience men, for example, have traditionally picked up from playing sports. We have all seen how that experience has played itself out time and time again in business. In my case, I relate well to my past experience from playing soccer and have made numerous connections to global business. But, at the same time, I would be the first to tell you that there are other ways for people to learn how a real team operates. Training is just one example."

Once again, Toni was reminded of her history lesson a few weeks ago with Grove. He had mentioned that soccer was regarded in the 1800s in Great Britain as a powerful force in the educational process. "Ron, you've answered my question."

"Great question, Toni."

"Ron, I think I'm beginning to really understand how soccer's operating principles connect to global business. If soccer was position-driven, for example, it would not make the same leadership and business connections we're talking about here. Right?"

"Yes! Bottom line, we're talking about relying on one another, along with emphasizing the team's success versus the individual's success," Ron said.

Indeed, as a former high school coach, Alex had spent most of his adult life dealing with the conflict between team versus individual success—or values. He had been part of a system that emphasized individual responsibility and performance over team performance. Alex saw soccer as an opportunity to reconcile the values conflict between individual performance and team performance. Historically, the conflict had always been an either/or argument, with the values presented as opposites on a continuum. However:

The reconciliation that soccer offered was not a question of dealing with the values in an either/ or application, but understanding that 'both' individual and team values are needed to compete.

In soccer and global business, this means placing the focus on results produced when all positions interact on the field. Individual accountability remains a critical ingredient in the process of producing the team's results. Individual players remain responsible for their skill development, which ultimately plays into or affects the team's development. The focus on individual development ultimately provides teams with the ability to determine what team skills are needed. This *cycle* of managing both individual and team development helps to ensure the process for producing team results is working.

"Dad, how are we doing for time?" Ron asked.

"I've got a few more minutes before I have to head off to the practice field."

"Good," Ron said.

"Let me also say that *multiple* skills are needed to play soccer," Alex continued. "Each player needs to be able to control the ball in the air and on the ground with both feet and the other parts of the body except for the hands, to change roles, and to play both offense and defense as the flow of the game dictates."

"Toni and I briefly talked about this earlier," Ron said.

"Then you really understand why a soccer player's ability to do many things reinforces the idea that soccer is not position-driven," Alex said. "In soccer, the need for people who are skilled and adaptable applies to both the individual and the team—who are expected to manage their entire work effort. In effect:

The soccer team is a self-directed unit charged with performing the work needing to be done.

"On top of that, the game is very fluid," Ron said, his eyes searching Toni's to ensure he was not over-whelming her with too much data at once. "It's played in a continuous tempo under changing conditions. If that doesn't sound like the global business model, I don't know what does!"

Toni agreed. "I can see why:

Skilled, adaptable people are needed in both soccer and global business.

"Soccer is also played on a larger field than most other sports," Alex said glancing over at Toni. "It requires that all players understand the bigger picture: team strategy, game-plan, goals, opponent's strengths and weaknesses, and more —all so important to the team's success. In summation:

Understanding the bigger picture 'empowers' all players on the field to make decisions, take risks, and manage and anticipate change as the flow of the game dictates.

"The soccer team," Ron continued, "is really a self-directed team operating on a real-time, continuous schedule. Individual players and the team must be able to respond to changing conditions on their own! Except for serious injury on the field, there are no opportunities to stop the game to plan a strategy, to give players a rest, or to slow down the opposition's momentum."

"Now that really sounds like global business." Toni remarked.

"When we talk about global business," Ron said, "we describe it as an interdependent network that is becoming increasingly decentralized. People working under this model are continuously challenged to make better decisions under changing conditions to compete. Here, the knowledge worker has certainly replaced the mass production worker of the past. Multi-skills, self-direction, and teamwork are the current and future realities."

"That's the game of soccer in a nutshell!" Alex said emphatically.

All of these characteristics, Toni realized, were representative of a *real* team and its current and future application in the global business world.

"Let me make one more point about soccer before I take off," Alex said. "People who have played soccer often have a good understanding of how to anticipate and manage change! Good soccer coaches teach people to look for the open space. That's where the opportunities exist for moving the ball up and down the field, maintain control on the field, and score goals. Being able to anticipate is a critical skill in playing soccer."

"What about people—like me—who have not played soccer? What does this mean?" Toni asked, challenging Ron.

"Good question," Ron said. "I believe by developing your knowledge of the game like we're doing, you will understand and become aware of what it means to anticipate, for example, on the business field. Hopefully, you can transfer this to your job performance, at least in the form of helping develop your business competencies. So playing the game is not the end-all here."

"Mind-set *before* skill-set sounds like the formula you're describing?" Toni asked.

"No question about it. We are building your commitment level for learning new competencies. Here we're talking about both organizational and job competencies."

"Can you give me an example?" she asked.

"Sure. Let's start with organizational competencies. There are a number of these that match up with each one of soccer's operating principles. For example, when we say 'focus on team—not position' competencies like 'adaptability' and 'learning agility' come to mind. Since we are using soccer's metaphor as a key part of our operating framework, that means our people need to be skilled in these *core* competencies to succeed in our team based business environment. Does that make sense?"

Toni nodded.

"Good. Let's talk about *job* competencies next. There are a number of these that match up with your new role as a global manager. 'Team management' is a prime example."

Toni laughed lightly. "No surprises there."

"Regardless of which competencies we talk about, the goal is to get you skilled in these competencies."

"Wow!" Toni said after saying goodbye to Alex. "Is he always that enthusiastic?"

"He can be. Especially if he gets talking about something he's passionate about like soccer."

"I see where you get your passion for soccer."

"Oh, yeah. His influence on me has been strong. That's partly why I continue to believe in soccer and its application in the global business world."

"Nick, let's go out tonight for dinner," Toni said as she walked through the door that evening.

"What do you have in mind?"

"Anything. How about Mexican?"

"That works for me. Let's go to Garcia's place."

After sipping a margarita Toni reluctantly said, "Guess what I did today?"

"What?" Nick said while glancing down at the menu.

"You're not much fun! I met with Tom Haas, the recruiter from Seattle, before I went to the office."

"No kidding!" he said, looking up from the menu. "How did it go? What did he say?"

"First he told me that his firm had targeted me as a candidate. He didn't say who he represented. He left me with a package of information including a job description and pay range. He said to give him a call if I'm interested. They have six months to fill the job."

"Anything else?"

"He seemed like a nice guy and was very professional. He also knew a lot about TAG and Ron in particular."

"That's his job. What did he say?"

"He said Ron was a good man, recognized for promoting all that 'team stuff' to use his words."

"That's interesting."

"Yeah, I thought so, too. He also said the company he represented was more 'traditional' in their management practices."

"Sounds like they don't have someone like Ron who is managing using team-based principles. Or they don't have a culture like TAG's."

"That's probably it," she said.

"My guess, maybe he threw that comment out there to get you thinking about the idea of working for a company with a more traditional culture."

"I've heard before that team-based cultures don't work for everyone," Toni said. "At least that's the argument."

"Okay. So how are you feeling? What are your thoughts?"

"I'm not really sure. Mixed emotions, I guess. On the one hand there are some attractive features about this opportunity. I would be working in domestic operations like before. I would be working in engineering, which is something I'm good at and enjoy. He led me to believe that I would be making more money than I did in my old job. He also mentioned that I would not have to deal with all the business travel, insinuating that it has been known to cause marital problems."

Nick maintained eye contact with Toni while taking in her feedback.

"On the other hand," Toni continued, "this would not be a good developmental opportunity for me. Becoming a manager is a short-term goal I've had for the past two years. That's why I accepted Ron's offer in the first place. My long-term goal is to run a global business, so working for Ron is a step in that direction. Also, his team-based strategy is working really well. Last but not least, my relationship with Ron is growing, and I think that's an important consideration for staying with TAG."

"I see you've really been thinking about things."

"That's why I wanted to go out tonight and talk. This can get to be a little overwhelming to say the least."

"I did say it was always good to keep your options open. I think so far you've done things in a professional way. However, you can't sit on the fence indefinitely. At some point you have to make a decision. If TAG is the direction that works for you at this point in your career, then stick with it. If not, perhaps this other opportunity is a viable option."

The Coach's Secret

"I am still thinking about what your father said last week," Toni said as she and Ron settled in for their long plane ride to Sao Paulo on Monday morning.

"We covered a lot of ground in a short time," Ron said. "This will be a good time to go over anything that needs clarifying."

"Nick and I were talking over the weekend about a number of things your father shared with me. For example, Nick wasn't clear on the idea that people who played soccer should be better at anticipating change. I wasn't able to explain it well either. If I can't explain it to Nick, I don't think I'll be able to discuss it with my team."

"Good point. And you're not the only one who doesn't understand it at first. Dad said teaching players to look for the open space in soccer is the key to winning games. It's the most effective way to move the ball up and down the field. Looking for the open space is another way to ask players to anticipate. The players who learn how to anticipate are considered the best players on the team and in their league. Obviously those teams that anticipate well are winning teams."

"So when you transfer the ability to anticipate 'what's up ahead' to the business world," Toni said, "you're suggesting that people will add value and be more effective in helping the business."

"Right. When we look at gaining a competitive advantage in business, being able to anticipate is huge! Especially when we're talking about anticipating change. That's construed as being *proactive* on the job. Those are the kind of people I want on my business team."

"Nick also liked what your father said about everybody being able to play soccer. He said it reminded him of how *everybody* today in business has the ability to access information on the Web."

"Exactly. All the technology we have at our disposal today really makes it possible for people everywhere to play in the global business world. And playing on the global business field really translates into being able to collaborate effectively in a variety of ways. In fact:

I see 'collaboration' associated with soccer in the same way that 'blocking and tackling' have been associated with American football!

"It really does sound like we're talking about one of soccer's operating principles," Toni said.

"No question about it," Ron said without hesitating. "Whether someone is playing on the soccer field or the global business field, people are continuously collaborating in numerous ways. In business, they're doing this in real time with information and knowledge, work and performance feedback."

"Again, I can relate."

"Anything else I need to clarify?" he asked.

"Not really. But I'm curious about your father. He didn't say much about himself. How long did he coach high school soccer? What were his coaching secrets?"

"Well, Dad's always been a pretty humble man, so he's never going to say much about himself. I think he coached high school soccer for about twenty-four years. Talking about his coaching secrets is probably a good way to talk about his leadership style."

"You did say a few weeks ago that soccer's metaphor represented the *best* example of leadership for global business."

"That's right," Ron said, laughing. "I'm glad you remembered!"

"After meeting your father how could I forget?"

"No argument there. Soccer is a game where the primary leadership style—or role—for the coach is to *delegate* and leave the execution of the game to the team. The continuous nature of the game dictates a limited role for the coach. As a delegating coach, this means the coach *empowers* the team to act independently from the coach during the game. This is reinforced through rules controlling the coach's behavior during the game, the limited number of substitutions a coach can make, and the referee. The coach's job during the game is to provide resources for the team to get the job done. This is really limited, however, during the game to providing the appropriate feedback from the bench and substituting a limited number of players, if necessary. During half-time, the coach has the opportunity to change leadership styles and be more directive when preparing the team for the second half of the game, if needed. However, in the end there is very little the coach can do to manage the team's efforts during the game. *The team's performance during the game is left up to the team."*

"That's why you describe it as a self-directed team," Toni said, smiling.

"Yes. When Dad coached, he would tell us that soccer was a players' game. It was our time to have fun since all he could do was delegate as a coach. He said his work was done at that point. Practice was his time or opportunity to teach and develop individual and team skills. He would use *different* leadership styles to teach both individual and team skills. It all depended on who he was working with and their skill level. Or in the case of the team, what game situation he was trying to teach and the team's skill level. So when you ask about Dad's coaching secrets, I think it all came down to his leadership!"

"Makes sense. I now understand why the delegating style is needed in soccer. The *continuous* nature of the game really dictates it, doesn't it? Interesting how your father changed leadership styles during practice. I was having a little trouble for a while trying to figure out how he taught the game to his players using only a delegating style."

"It's an important distinction to make. When you look at *how* I have tried to teach you these operating principles, I have used a few leadership styles along the way. For example, in preparing your transition plan, I was highly directive in describing my expectations for your development. When we started meeting after your return from vacation, I gave you a history lesson or two to help build your commitment for learning *why* soccer's metaphor works in today's global economy. That communications exchange represented a shift in my leadership style. In my absence, Grove attempted to do the same thing, demonstrating added support for building your understanding. Does that make sense?"

"I think so. I could see how you were less directive and more supportive in how you both communicated with me. Especially when you were asking me questions. The dialogue was more two-way than one-way."

"This has been our practice time when you think about it! Eventually, we will get to a point where I'll turn things over to you. At that point, I will be delegating."

"Thanks for helping me absorb all this," Toni said. "The soccer coach does provide the best description of what leadership looks like for people and teams working in global business. As you said earlier:

The global business world has become more and more like soccer.

"In contrast to the leadership style of the soccer coach," said Ron, "one typically finds the football coach in a *directing* leadership style during the game. The head coach is like a general and his assistant coaches are like captains and lieutenants, to use a military analogy. During the game coaches are constantly developing strategies, scripting plays, changing players, calling time-outs, and the like to win the battle—or game. Special units with specialized players are established to address game situations like offense, defense, and kicking. Within each of those special units are sub-units with specialized players. For example, there are kicking specialists to address kickoffs to start a game, kicks for extra points, and kicks for field goals. Because the game is not a continuous game and it is position-driven, the coach and his staff play an active role throughout the game. Again, this is described as a directing leadership style."

"Big difference than soccer," Toni said.

"You can see this on TV on any Saturday or Sunday afternoon

during the fall. Here we see the television camera constantly shifting back and forth from the playing field —focusing on the quarterback—to the head coach on the sideline—to the assistant coach in the press-box—who are all wired with headsets to coordinate their thinking and planning for the next play of the game. In fact, today most quarterbacks don't even call the plays anymore like they did when Dad grew up watching Bart Starr or Johnny Unitas. Quarterbacks now have headsets in their helmets to hear the coaches call plays. Meanwhile, players from both teams constantly enter and exit the game. In this scenario, the team is totally dependent upon the head coach and his staff for executing the game plan. One could argue that the coaches are more responsible for the execution since they are trying to control the flow of the game with their involvement."

"It almost sounds like remote control," Toni said.

"I don't want to beat this metaphor to death, but it is important to recognize the significance of leadership to global business. In looking at today's global business model, we all recognize that it is a growing interdependent network. It requires leadership that is far different from the hierarchical command and control or highly directive style. Again, the successful soccer coach provides the best description of effective leadership for a team application in the global business. He or she is someone who has faith in individuals and teams to accept responsibility for getting the work done! This calls for someone who can effectively delegate over time, yet demonstrate the flexibility to change leadership styles, when required, to address changing needs."

"That's exactly what we talked about earlier in describing the soccer coach who played a delegating role during the game," Toni said confidently. "In contrast, during practice the coach changes leadership styles to meet the development needs of the individuals and the team."

"We're also talking about a coach who has a strong *service* orientation," Ron continued. "Last but not least, we're talking about a leader whose ego is left in check. I'm sure there are other characteristics I can add to this list, but you get the gist of what I'm describing."

"I don't think you're belaboring the point," Toni said. "I didn't know anything about either American football or soccer before I got my new job. The comparison has helped me really understand why the soccer coach represents a better fit for what leadership looks like in global business. And to tell you the truth, I'd far rather be a soccer coach than a football coach."

Ron leaned back and grinned. "Glad to hear it. In the end, we have to remember that leadership is an *influence* process. Accepting leadership as a process requires acknowledging that a viable relationship or partnership exists between the soccer coach— or business manager—and players on the team. Without that understanding you don't have effective leadership."

Achieving Cross-Cultural Agility

"You look like you didn't get much sleep," Carlos said as he approached Ron in the hotel lobby.

"Thanks, Carlos. I needed to hear that," Ron said, extending his hand to greet him.

"How was the flight?"

"Good. Our connection in Dallas was close, but we made it okay."

"Any schedule changes since Friday?"

"No. I'll meet with Ricardo at ten o'clock this morning to deal with his concerns. I think it's going to be one of those meetings that could be very short or very long—nothing in between if you know what I mean. Hopefully, it's short and we can move on."

"Are you still planning to return to the States when you wrap things up?"

"Yes. I need to get back to help Grove with the Rome

project. He's filling in for Anthony Burgamo in Italy, who was unexpectedly hospitalized two weeks ago. I think Anthony will be out of commission for about six weeks."

"Sounds serious."

"He broke his ankle. He's playing it down, but he'll need surgery. Nothing life threatening, but I feel for him."

Ron smiled as he saw Toni approach and turned his attention to her. "Carlos, meet Toni Burns," Ron said, reaching out to draw Toni into their group.

"Nice to meet you," said Toni as she shook Carlos' hand.

"Welcome to Sao Paulo and Brazil. Is this your first trip here?" Carlos asked with a big grin.

"Yes. I'm looking forward to our visit even though it's a short one. I hope there's at least a bit of time for some sight–seeing."

"I'll make sure of it," Carlos said. "You know what they say about all work and no play."

Ron and Toni both laughed.

"Carlos, let's grab a bite to eat before we hit the road," Ron said walking toward the café entrance inside the hotel. "We didn't get a chance to eat when we got in last night. I'm starving."

Carlos Rio was one of Ron's newer hires. He had come on board four years earlier after working six years for a competitor in both Central America and Argentina. He had gone to work for the competition straight out of college, armed with his engineering degree. Since he only had limited managerial experience, Ron mentored Carlos regularly the first couple of years on the job. Carlos had responded well to Ron's mentoring and was now a solid manager with good interpersonal and leadership skills. He was well respected by his team in Sao Paulo. For the most part Ron now delegated most things to Carlos when it came to business in this part of the world.

"What's the plan for the day?" Toni asked as they sat down for breakfast.

"Carlos is taking me to Ricardo's office. My guess, I will probably spend the balance of the day with Ricardo. It may include dinner. That will give you and Carlos the chance to get to know each other. We'll touch base later when I know more."

"Ron tells me that you've been learning all about our approach to managing the business," Carlos said after dropping Ron off.

"It's been very interesting to learn why it's needed and how Ron has made it work here at TAG," Toni said.

"As you probably know, soccer in this country is part of our national character. So making his metaphor work for us has been a good fit. Its application really helps people on my team, for example, understand what teamwork looks like on a day-to-day basis."

"Can you tell me more about how it helps your team?"

"Well, for one thing," Carlos said, taking a deep breath,

"soccer helps everyone understand that we must all find ways to collaborate with each other. The idea that we are all players on the same team is well understood and accepted."

"So, if I asked everyone on your team if they are an interdependent part of the team, they would understand and agree?"

"Of course. My team really works like a soccer team. That's our operating framework or model. I am very fortunate to have good people on the team. Most of the time, my job is to stay out of their way and let them perform."

"So you function like a soccer coach?"

"For sure. I even tell them to consider me their soccer coach so they all understand my role helping the team."

"How much of their understanding comes from soccer being a part of your national character or culture versus any training that you've provided?"

"Soccer in this country and many countries in this part of the world is deeply ingrained in our communities. One may argue that our people are more passionate about soccer than religion. That is not for me to say. So the answer to your question is tied to the fact that soccer is a big part of our national character. Understanding comes from this. At the same time, when I train and coach my people, I deliberately use Ron's metaphor to help build understanding around his business approach to managing the team. I think it really resonates with my people."

"How about your coaching methods? What can you share with me about how you lead your team?"

"Ron's been helpful to me there. For example, he sent me to a leadership training class in San Francisco during my first year in this job where I learned how to effectively lead people. The training was all about being able to change leadership styles to fit the needs of my people. Since then, I have sent all members of my team through the training. We now have a *common* language about what effective leadership looks like, especially what it means to effectively delegate! This has been very powerful. It all makes our team communications much easier."

Before responding, Toni made a note that she needed to ask Ron about the leadership training Carlos had mentioned.

"So how do you feel about Ron promoting the application of soccer to our business?" Toni asked.

"I'm not sure I understand your question," Carlos said, puzzled.

"Okay. Let me try asking it this way. TAG is an American company doing business all over the world. Ron is using a metaphor based on a game that historically has belonged to the rest of the world, not really to the U.S. What do you think about this?"

"It's great," Carlos said passionately. "It says a lot about his interest to build a more *inclusive* team culture in the company. It also says a lot about TAG Industries' commitment to create a company culture that transcends multicultural differences. He likes to describe this as a way to help:

Achieve Cross-Cultural Agility

"Ron shared that with me a few weeks ago," Toni said. "I wasn't sure I understood what he meant at the time, but talking with you makes it clearer."

"Glad to hear it."

Toni smiled at Carlos. "So, the use of this metaphor really resonates with you and your team. I picked up the same feelings talking to Grove when he was in the office a few weeks ago."

"I'm not surprised to hear that. I've worked with Grove from time to time. He's an avid supporter of its use in international business. I've also traveled all through Europe during my university years and would say the same things about Europe's passion for the game. It really becomes a way to connect and establish a relationship with people on *both* a personal level and a business level."

"Did you play soccer?" Toni asked.

"Yes. I still play with some friends."

"How about the people on your business team? Have they all played?"

"Most of them have played at some level over the years. A couple of others haven't played, but they have a good understanding of how soccer relates to our work—if that's what you're asking?"

"My line of questioning is fairly obvious," Toni said, smiling.

"That's okay. You're trying to learn. Also remember, as part of the team we all help each other, so ask me as many questions as you want."

After a late lunch Carlos and Toni met Carlos' team and talked with a customer who was in the office to finalize job specs for a project in central Brazil. To their surprise, Ron had called and left a message around mid-afternoon, saying he would meet them back at the hotel for dinner that evening.

"That was quick work," Toni greeted Ron when she and Carlos met him later for dinner.

"The meeting was cut short," Ron said. "Ricardo had a last minute meeting with a government official he couldn't miss. So we're on board again tomorrow morning at ten o'clock."

"How was his demeanor?" Carlos asked.

"Not too bad. He bought lunch if that means anything. I think he may be testing our mettle. You don't know this Toni, but when we were awarded this job, the president of TAG Industries personally committed 'yours truly' to the project. Otherwise Carlos would have handled this with Ricardo."

Carlos nodded.

"So how was your day?" asked Ron as they sat down for dinner.

"Great," said Toni. "I had the chance to see a little more of the city, meet Carlos' team, and I even met a customer who was in the office finalizing some paperwork for a job in central Brazil."

"The Brasilia Project," Carlos said, smiling.

"Right," Ron said. "That's another important project for us. Good work on wrapping that one up, Carlos."

"Thanks. So far it's been a lot of fun working with those people. The project could do amazing things economically in that part of my country—and God knows people there have had it rough financially for a long time now."

The three sat quietly while the waiter set their food in front of them. When he left, Ron turned to Toni. "What was the best part of your day?"

She laughed. "You're going to think I'm trying to butter you up, but I swear I'm telling the truth. My favorite part was learning more about soccer from Carlos. He really helped me understand how soccer helps achieve cross-cultural agility in the business. I know we briefly talked about that a few weeks ago, but I didn't pretend to understand what that meant. Now I think I honestly get it."

"Achieving cross-cultural agility is a very tricky landscape to manage," Ron said. "The metaphor's application here is just a *small* way of helping people and business make that transition more successful." Ron took a bite of his salad. "Wouldn't you agree Carlos?"

"Very much so. Even here in South America, managing across cultures can be challenging. There are a number of differences between many of the countries on this continent. For example, language is a basic difference between Brazil and Argentina. But soccer's metaphor does provide us with a global vision of how we are expected to work as a team here in Brazil, South America, and around the globe."

"Most of the research I've seen in this area," Ron said, "would point out that there are at least *five* major areas to address in helping global teams succeed: senior management's leadership role, the innovative use of communications technology, adoption of an organization design that enhances global operations, prevalence of trust among team members, and the ability to capture the strengths of diverse cultures, languages, and people. That's a big, big list when you think about it!"

"I think Ron's idea of applying soccer to our business is perfect," said Carlos. "Not only does it provide an organizing framework for the team, it has helped establish a common bond and trust. I can't speak for all for all regions, but I know Grove feels this way. Last, and perhaps most important, I think because of senior management's commitment to the use of soccer, we are able to tap into the strengths of everyone on the team. So by my count we're hitting on most of the areas Ron mentioned!"

"Thanks, Carlos," Ron said. "I would reaffirm the importance of having the capability of tapping into everyone's strengths. That plays into our ability to effectively *collaborate* as a team on the global business field with others, including our customers."

"Carlos talked earlier about the need to collaborate in the business," Toni said.

"I'm not surprised," said Ron. "Both Carlos and Grove see it the same way. In fact, they both like to describe our soccer metaphor as a:

Strategic Operating Collaboration
Code *for* Engaging Resources

"It definitely promotes resource collaboration when you put all the pieces together," Toni said.

Ron reached for his water. "It really does. I've found that engagement increases tremendously when we communicate in a language that people understand."

"And soccer offers that language!" Carlos said.

"I also like to tell Carlos and Grove that our metaphor serves as a:

Strategic Operating Collaboration
Code *for* Earning Results

"That's my way of pushing back and having some fun with these guys, keeping the team focused on the bottom line."

"I tell my customers," Carlos said, "that 'soccer' also stands for:

Strategic Operating Collaboration

Code *for* Establishing Relationships

"So do I have to come up with something, too?" Toni asked.
Ron and Carlos laughed.

"Don't lose any sleep over it," Carlos said, smiling.

"Carlos, let me add," Ron said, "that all of the regions across our global network feel the same as you about how soccer has helped to establish a common bond and trust. In time Toni will get exposure to her global team. I'm optimistic that she'll come away with the same feelings you've shared tonight."

"Carlos also shared some good comments with me earlier today about the company's commitment to transcend multicultural differences," Toni added. "That says a lot about the leadership at the senior level of the company!"

"It really does when you think about it from a strategic standpoint," Ron said. "As global leaders, we need to find ways to create multicultural communities in organizations. Soccer helps to achieve this by providing people in organizations with what some call beacons—values and attitudes—that are comprehensible to employees across cultures."

Play On

Wednesday morning the phone startled Toni awake. She hadn't asked for a wake-up call, so she struggled for a moment trying to gather her thoughts before picking up the phone.

"Hi, Toni," Ron whispered, his voice barely recognizable. "It appears Carlos and I picked up food poisoning. How are you?"

"Fine."

"Good. Carlos and I ate the same thing last night. There's your common denominator." He paused while he battled a wave of stomach cramps. When they passed, he continued, "The hotel is taking me over to the local hospital to be examined. Carlos is already on his way to see his doctor."

"What about your meeting today with Ricardo?"

"There's no way that I can make it! I have to assume the same holds true for Carlos. You'll have to step in for us on this one."

Toni's stomach lurched. Although Ron had briefed her about the issue on the plane, she didn't feel ready to take something over. "Can't the meeting be rescheduled for tomorrow? I'll be happy to call and take care of that. I'm sure you'll be fine tomorrow."

"Ricardo's leaving for Europe for ten days. We have to get the issue resolved before he leaves. Sorry, Toni, there aren't any other options. I have confidence you can handle the situation. We have to 'play on' as they say in soccer."

"Okay. I'll do my best."

"Thanks, Toni. I'll call Ricardo's office and tell him you'll be filling in for me. You'll do just fine."

Sitting in the hospital was not something that appealed to Ron at any time, especially now. It was like sitting on the sidelines during a soccer game. He had been conditioned to be a player in both soccer—and business. Not being a part of the action was new, and he didn't much like it.

He knew meeting with Ricardo on her own would be challenging for Toni. On the one hand, her engineering background coupled with her strong interpersonal skills, would serve as a solid foundation in her dealings with him. But on the other hand, Ron was concerned about her credibility with Ricardo. Being the rookie on the team was something that he would pick up on quickly. He was not sure how that would play-out in their negotiations.

Toni's head spun with all kinds of possibilities as she stepped into the cab. What if she didn't connect with Ricardo? What if she failed to convince him the company could effectively deal with the issue? What if she didn't have the answers he was looking for? The list went on and on…

"Destination? Destination?" the cab driver repeated impatiently.

"I'm sorry, 1256 San Marcos Boulevard."

Thoughts of contacting Tom Haas entered her mind as the cab made its way to Ricardo's office. She tried to get these thoughts out of her head. Right now, she had to focus on the issue at hand and anticipate questions he may ask. The issue had to do with one of the company's new plants supplying engineered products that failed to meet Ricardo's specifications. Currently, TAG supplied these products to Ricardo's firm from five plants across the globe. His people assembled them into a finished product. Ricardo was looking for answers regarding how to deal with what he called a "weak link" in the system. The problem, if not fixed immediately, could cost him delays with contractors. The delays would end up becoming back-charges for TAG. Things could get very expensive quickly!

"You can come in now," said the young lady from behind the desk. "Mr. Aurelio is waiting to see you."

"Thank you."

"Good morning. I'm Ricardo Aurelio," he said, walking over to greet her.

"I'm Toni Burns. Very nice to meet you."

"Please have a seat. May I get you anything?"

"No thanks, I'm fine for now."

"Good. Ron and I met for a few hours yesterday. Most of what we accomplished consisted of verifying that your product shipped to us from your plant in South Korea was not meeting our quality specifications. We agreed that it may be a product 'fit for service,' but it did not meet the specifications that were drawn up in the contract. My argument is that the probabilities of 'this' product failing are higher than a product that meets our quality specifications. Because it's a product used to transport clean water to our cities and is constantly under high pressure, we cannot afford to accept the product."

"Ron briefed me on the plane coming down."

"Good, so we understand each other."

"We do," Toni said, shifting in her chair.

"How do you propose resolving the problem?"

"Ron said you have enough inventory to keep you on schedule with your contractors for the next thirty days. We can supply you with product from one or two other plants. In fact, we can supply you with product from both of those plants, if necessary, to get your inventory up to acceptable levels."

"So what happened at your South Korean plant?"

"We're continuing to look for answers. According to Ron, we have been in the process of transitioning that plant into our company culture. It's only been under our ownership for four months. We purchased it from a competitor."

"I see. I wasn't aware of that."

"TAG Industries has a strong culture that helps us avoid these kinds of problems. Unfortunately, we're playing catch–up getting this plant operating up to our standards."

"Tell me more about your culture. This is my first contract with your company. Other than finances, I know little about how your company operates."

"As you know, we are global. We have a network of plant operations that make it possible for us to be a global partner with people like yourself. Ron likes to describe this as his 'collaboration' strategy. He promotes teamwork along with operating principles like diversity, interdependence, empowerment, and cross-cultural agility."

"How does he do all of that?"

"Ron believes a successful business team is a lot like a successful soccer team. He's created a series of operating principles for the company that mirror what happens on the soccer field."

Ricardo nodded. "Interesting."

"As you probably know, outside of the U.S., soccer represents a universal language—and soccer is coming into its own in the U.S. now as well! Ron has been successful in leveraging that in the business. It's really helped to build trust, for example, across our teams so that we can effectively collaborate with each other and our customers. This is a prime example of what I'm talking about."

"I understand what you are saying. I have played a little football—or soccer—as you call it. Those connections are real. I especially like what you are trying to do with the idea of achieving cross-cultural agility. I would think that would be the biggest challenge for Ron and the company."

"Carlos told me yesterday that Ron has been working on building a culture that transcends multicultural differences for some time. He says soccer's application to the business really resonates with his team. I heard the same thing a few weeks ago when I talked to our European manager."

"I am not surprised to hear what Carlos had to say. Our culture is very group oriented. Soccer works well here in Brazil, as it does in many cultures around the world."

"That's exactly what Ron said."

"I understand that you are fairly new in your role with the company?"

"Yes," Toni said reluctantly. "I've been in my new role for about six weeks. Before that I was a project engineer."

"You appear to really understand Ron's business philosophy and have bought into it."

"Is that a question, Mr. Aurelio?"

"No, more of an observation than anything. And, please, call me Ricardo!"

"I am still learning how Ron operates. I have a long way to go before I get to his level of understanding."

"This is all new for me as well."

"How so?" Toni asked.

"Most of my encounters with others have not been as productive as this one. I often see other firms come in here and offer little flexibility to help solve business problems. They tend to dictate solutions—if you know what I mean. Ron and now you, describe an approach I have not seen before. You used the term 'collaboration' earlier. That approach is what makes you different, and I think that's good. I like what I am hearing. It makes for a good partnership."

The balance of Toni's meeting with Ricardo appeared to go without a hitch. He even insisted on taking Toni for a late lunch before saying goodbye. During lunch he indicated he would contact Ron directly to determine his next steps.

Toni was not sure—or really confident enough—to know how things ended up with Ricardo as she headed back to the hotel that afternoon. Again, thoughts of contacting Tom Haas returned. As much as she tried to squelch these thoughts, she found it hard to do so. If things did not work out with Ricardo, perhaps she would have to contact Tom. She even found herself thinking that she may contact him regardless of how things turned out with Ricardo. Maybe this whole thing about becoming a manager of a global business team, using soccer's metaphor, was too much of a stretch for her.

That evening Ron called to say he was feeling a little better. He told her briefly that he'd spoken with Ricardo and would fill her in tomorrow on the plane. They agreed to meet at six o'clock in the morning to grab a cab to the airport.

Toni hoped her nerves would hold out that long.

The Never-Ever Ending

Toni spent the night in her room going over the details of her meeting with Ricardo. She replayed everything over and over, trying to figure out if she had made the right choices and said the right things. She tried in vain to reach Nick to talk things over with him. Her frustration level was pretty high by the time she finally fell asleep.

Wondering how Ron felt about the outcome of her meeting with Ricardo was foremost on Toni's mind the next morning as they headed to the airport. Ron appeared to be feeling better, but he didn't say much along the way. She reminded herself to be patient and follow Nick's advice to "trust" Ron's leadership.

Collecting her thoughts as she got settled in for the long return trip to Portland, Toni made note of her list of leader characteristics. In her journal she added eight more items to her list that she picked up from talking with Ron and Carlos:

LEADER CHARACTERISTICS:

Decisive
Pro-active
Gives Credit
Passionate
Team Builder
Humble-Humility
Insightful
Ego In Check
Strategic

Overall, she was impressed with how consistent everyone was in their leadership of both people and the business. She saw a number of the same leader characteristics in Carlos that both Ron and Grove exhibited. She was sure that would hold true for the rest of her team. After all, Ron and Grove had said as much. Ron had put together an impressive group of people. Obviously, he was instrumental in setting the direction for his team. Yet at the same time, they all expressed a sincere—and passionate—desire to work as a team with soccer's metaphor serving as a guide on their journey. Very impressive, she thought.

"I'm back," Ron said, as he sat down next to Toni.

"Feeling any better?"

"Yeah. I think I've turned the corner. I may even be able to eat something. Hopefully we won't have to wait long for a meal."

"Are you up to talking about your conversation last night with Ricardo?" Toni asked, smiling nervously.

"This should be a good time. First, let me say that I didn't mean to keep you hanging out there. That food poisoning really wiped me out. I couldn't believe how tired I was last night."

Toni nodded.

"As I mentioned on the phone, Ricardo and I spoke briefly last night. He was satisfied with all the suggestions you made, including having one of our other plants pick up the needed production. He and Grove are going to work out the details in a couple of days when Ricardo is in Europe. Grove will be meeting him in Rome."

"You mean *collaborating* with him!"

"Not bad, not bad," Ron said, laughing. "What else can I tell you?"

"Well, we talked about a number of things I thought were important for him to know: our collaboration strategy, company culture, and the like. How did that come across?"

"He felt like you went out of your way to establish a relationship with him. He was impressed with how you expressed yourself. He really liked what you had to say about collaborating with his firm. He was surprised to learn that we used the soccer metaphor as part of our operating framework. He even asked if you had played soccer!"

"You're kidding!"

"No. I told him that you knew little about soccer before you took on your new job."

"That's interesting."

"Toni, I know it's only a beginning, but you certainly got off to a great start with him."

"That's wonderful! I wasn't really sure how things ended up with him yesterday."

"Let's just say you connected! In today's global business world, *relationships* are extremely important."

"As you recall, Carlos said the same thing," Toni said, confidently. "He talked about how soccer enabled him and others on his team to establish relationships with customers and others, including teams across our network at TAG."

"And that can be a hard lesson to learn," Ron said. "Many of us have a tendency to discount the importance of relationships in business. Especially in our hard-charging, task-oriented business environment in the U.S. You know the rest of the story."

"I sure do."

"We must all learn to become *people* architects, finding creative ways to build and bridge relationships with people across our business."

"I can honestly say I now understand first-hand how soccer helps us connect with people."

In the short time Toni had been on board in her new job, Ron had seen solid growth on her part. He knew her commitment for learning everything in her new job—including her comprehension of soccer's metaphor—was increasing with each passing day. He was encouraged.

"I meant to ask you about a training program Carlos mentioned," Toni asked Ron as they were finishing up breakfast on the flight home.

"He probably told you about the program in San Francisco he went to about three years ago."

"That was it!"

"We have you scheduled for that same program in four weeks. It's a great program. It'll teach you how to effectively lead your people by learning to *change* your leadership style to fit the needs of your people."

"That's just how Carlos described it."

"If you recall, we talked earlier about leadership being an 'influence' process."

"I remember. That was when you were describing the leadership differences between a soccer coach and a football coach."

"Exactly. Being able to effectively influence your people is an important 'job' competency that you must have in your 'skills' portfolio as a global manager!"

"So this program really matches up well to that specific developmental need," Toni said.

"It sure does. Besides Carlos, Grove and all of our regional managers have gone through the program. I believe most of their people have been trained as well."

"That's great. I can't wait to go through the training. It sounds like a class your father could teach."

"Perhaps. It certainly fits well with his approach to leading people."

"Carlos said it was a powerful learning experience and made it a lot easier for him to communicate with his team. He also said the training provided a common language for the team."

"He's right. The training does just that. It also provides him with a foundation or platform to help his people grow, ensuring that the process for producing team results is working. This is especially true in today's global business world."

"How so?"

"Its purpose is to help leaders like Carlos become aware of which leadership style to use to help develop his people. It can be a significant resource in enabling him to function as an increasingly knowledgeable and insightful leader for his people. This all leads to the issue of motivating his people, and we all know that:

Motivation represents a 'gray matter' for all of us. It is energy that, once seen or experienced, is perhaps the ultimate intangible in helping individuals, teams, and organizations achieve results.

"Dad was a firm believer in finding all kinds of ways to tap into this energy source. When he coached soccer he had his own system for motivating and inspiring his players. He was also big on the *relationship* side of things. He believed first in establishing and maintaining relationships with all of his players. He would say:

We all know a manager or coach whose

success is dependent upon his or her ability to

transcend technique and deal with people

on a relationship basis.

"I can appreciate that now after meeting your father," Toni said. "He would be someone most people could connect with pretty easily."

"Dad used to also say that the skills needed to be an effective leader in business, government, education, and soccer are the same. Again, I think he's right."

"Meaning that a leader—is a leader—is a leader," Toni said confidently. "The common denominator is *people*, and most leaders struggle with the same kinds of issues: how to motivate and inspire their people—both individuals and teams—to produce results."

"By the way Toni, I have you scheduled for a trip with me right after you complete your leadership class. We can plan to meet in San Francisco and fly over to our offices in China and India. We can also visit the South Korean plant to learn more about its problems. This will give you the opportunity to see that part of the world and meet your regional managers in both countries."

"Wow! So far this has been a challenging journey for me,

to say the least!"

"My plan," Ron said reassuringly, "is to continue to provide you with the appropriate leadership to help you succeed in your new role. That includes continuing to coach you on soccer's application in the business."

They both nodded.

"Speaking of the journey, at this point we have covered all of soccer's operating principles I shared with you a number of weeks ago. Those were:

SOCCER'S GLOBAL BUSINESS OPERATING PRINCIPLES:

1. Focus On Team—Not Position
2. Understand That Everybody Can Play
3. Embrace Diversity
4. Rely On Each Other
5. Promote Both Individual and Team Values
6. Seek Skillful, Adaptable Players
7. Charge The Team To Perform The Work
8. Empower Players To Win
9. Coach Teams To Respond To Changing Conditions On Their Own
10. Develop Partners On The Field
11. Achieve Cross-Cultural Agility

"My job has been to teach you how soccer can help you and your team be successful in the global business world. Along the way, I have asked others on our team to help with your education and training. I think we have a solid foundation in place. Are you comfortable with this so far?"

"My confidence is definitely growing. You, Grove, your father, and Carlos have all been very good teammates in 'coaching' me on your approach to managing the business. I really feel like I have a good understanding of the operating principles. Also, I'm convinced that the global business world has become more and more like soccer!"

"I'm glad you feel that way. I'm sure the others do, too."

"That's good to hear."

"Toni, our challenge moving forward is to continue to build your knowledge of these operating principles. The best way to do this is to build your skills in those organizational and job competencies we discussed last week. That way we will have you better positioned to realize the operating principles."

"I like that game plan!"

"I thought you would." Handing her a piece of paper, Ron added, "These are the *key* organizational competencies we talked about last week that match up with soccer's global operating principles. There may be others that we add later, but this will get us started:

SOCCER'S GLOBAL BUSINESS

OPERATING PRINCIPLES

Competencies

1. Focus On Team—Not Position

- *Adaptability*
- *Learning Agility*
- *Relationship Building*
- *Team Management*
- *Team Player*

2. Understand That Everybody Can Play

- *Energy*
- *Initiative*
- *Technical Expertise*

3. Embrace Diversity

- *Global Skills*
- *Relationship Building*
- *Sensitivity*

4. Rely On Each Other

- *Relationship Building*
- *Team Management*
- *Team Player*

5. Promote Both Individual and Team Values

- *Global Skills*
- *Integrity*
- *Relationship Building*
- *Sensitivity*

6. Seek Skillful, Adaptable Players

- *Adaptability*
- *Learning Agility*
- *Organizing and Planning*
- *Technical Expertise*

7. Charge The Team To Perform The Work

- *Customer Orientation*
- *Results Orientation*
- *Visioning*

8. Empower Players To Win

- *Problem Solving and Decision Making*
- *Risk Taking*

9. Coach Teams To Respond To Changing Conditions On Their Own

- *Mission Focus*
- *Strategic Thinking*

10. Develop Partners On The Field

- *Active Communication*
- *Coaching and Counseling*
- *Delegation*
- *Influence*
- *Relationship Building*

11. Achieve Cross-Cultural Agility

- *Global Skills*
- *Learning Agility*
- *Relationship Building*
- *Self Objectivity*

"As you can see, there are twenty-four organizational competencies listed. Eight of these competencies connect with a number of the operating principles. On the backside of the page, I've listed the top eight competencies, showing their application to the principles:

TOP EIGHT COMPETENCIES:

Relationship Building = 6 out of 11 principles

Learning Agility = 3 out of 11 principles

Global Skills = 3 out of 11 principles

Adaptability = 2 out of 11 principles

Team Management = 2 out of 11 principles

Team Player = 2 out of 11 principles

Technical Expertise = 2 out of 11 principles

Sensitivity = 2 out of 11 principles

"I can add that 'relationship building' could actually apply to eight out of eleven operating principles."

"It definitely reinforces what your father said about relationships coming first in dealing with people."

"Especially in global business. Despite the fact that we have laid out a framework of eleven operating principles and a host of complementary organizational and job competencies, in the end it really comes down to understanding that global leadership may be more about art than science—with *relationships* being key."

Toni nodded, thinking of her list of "leader characteristics" and how they served as the *foundation* for establishing relationships. Obviously, Ron, Grove, and Carlos were highly effective managers who embodied these characteristics.

"Here's another point worth making," Ron said. "A number of the competencies deal with the need to be *flexible* and *responsive* to changing needs." Competencies like learning agility, adaptability, global skills, sensitivity, and self objectivity fall into that category."

"Looks like I have some work to do," Toni said.

"We both do. Developing your skills in organizational competencies, where needed, is all part of the development plan we initially talked about. The good news is that you already have adequate skills in a number of these competencies. So we're not starting from scratch here."

Toni agreed.

"How about 'job' competencies?" she asked. "Other than the influence and team management competencies we talked about earlier, what remaining job competencies do I need to develop?"

"More good news here," said Ron with a slight grin. "A number of organization competencies listed under the operating principles overlap most of the key job competencies for your role as a global manager. Competencies like relationship building, problem solving and decision making, organizing and planning, and active communications go hand in hand with influence and team management as being key competencies in your new role. There may be others we add in the future. For now, I think we can get the most leverage concentrating on the 'top eight' competencies from the list of organizational competencies."

"Sounds like a good strategy."

"We can start focusing on how to tackle this challenge next week. On Monday, I'll send you a detailed description of the behaviors associated with each competency.[1] That way you will have a chance to review these before we meet on Wednesday."

Toni nodded.

"One last thought," Ron said reflectively. "Before we close this chapter in your journey, I'm confident you now understand and accept that your:

Leadership development is a journey
with a never-ever ending!

---

[1] See Appendix

Epilogue

Sitting back in her seat on the plane, Toni reflected on what Ron said about Ricardo's feedback, his interest in mapping competencies to soccer's operating principles, the importance of relationships to success in global business, and her future training plans. She was impressed with the development plan he had put together for her. Ron had done a great job of *connecting* all the dots.

Although he admitted that it may be easy for her to get overwhelmed by the number of competencies, he was convinced they would provide her with a *learning* focus to help her *realize* the operating principles. She agreed. She was also convinced that his way of running the business, using soccer's metaphor, was an excellent match for the global business economy.

As she started to close her eyes, Toni was relieved that she had come through for Ron and the company. She felt good about her new role, her ability to make the transition to becoming a global business leader, and her relationship with Ron. She was eager to get home and tell Nick that her "fence-riding" days were over.

"Tom, this is Toni Burns," she said calmly while sitting in her office on Monday morning.

"Toni. Hi. How are you?"

"Fine, thank you. Tom, I wanted to get back to you on our earlier conversation."

"Great."

"The opportunity you've presented sounds great, but I realize that the TAG job is a growth step—although maybe a scary one. The job you described is more of what I have already done. I also believe that to thrive a global business has to be led in almost an entirely different way, and I am signing up for Ron's way of running the business. Thanks very much for considering me for the opportunity."

"Toni, thank you for getting back to me on your decision. I wish you all the best."

Monday afternoon Ron came by and greeted Toni with a big grin. In his hands was a gold-plated cup with a soccer ball sitting on top. Engraved on the side of the cup was the number "11."

Toni had seen a similar ornament in Carlos' office and thought it was a trophy he earned while playing soccer in Brazil.

"What's this all about?" she asked, surprised.

"I wanted to officially congratulate you on your accomplishments in learning how to become a manager of a global business team. Obviously that includes learning how soccer's "11" operating principles can help you manage your team."

"Wow! I'm honored."

"You should be. I usually present this cup to individuals once they complete all the steps in their development plan. In your case, your efforts so far to make the transition successful have been outstanding! Both Grove and Carlos recommended that we do this as well. So, from all three of us—congratulations!"

Appendix

OPERATING PRINCIPLES

COMPETENCIES

**RELATED
BEHAVIORS,
SKILLS and
ATTRIBUTES**

OPERATING PRINCIPLE # 1: *Focus* **On Team—Not Position**

COMPETENCIES: Adaptability, Learning Agility, Relationship Building, Team Player, Team Management

RELATED BEHAVIORS, SKILLS and ATTRIBUTES:

Adaptability	Are flexible and open to new ideas; are quick to adapt to new situations.
Learning Agility	Rapidly assimilate and use new information; seek new knowledge; foster a learning environment.
Relationship Building	Recognize importance of relationships; devote energy to cultivating relationships; enjoy being around people; maintain broad internal and external networks of business relationships.
Team Player	Share resources toward organizational goals; truly appreciate the synergy that teamwork can provide-the whole is often greater than the sum of the parts; actively communicate and build relationships with other team members.
Team Management	Identify team roles; set and communicate team goals; monitor team progress towards goals; actively work to maintain team focus; foster team atmosphere and reward collaboration.

OPERATING PRINCIPLE # 2: *Understand* **That Everybody Can Play**

COMPETENCIES: Energy, Initiative, Technical Expertise

RELATED BEHAVIORS, SKILLS, and ATTRIBUTES:

Energy	Exhibit stamina, endurance; are hard workers; continue to produce in exhausting conditions; maintain fast pace over time.
Initiative	Take action without being prompted; provide unsolicited input; are proactive, not reactive.
Technical Expertise	Exhibit functional knowledge, bring unique expertise, maintain current technical skills.

OPERATING PRINCIPLE # 3: ***Embrace* Diversity**

COMPETENCIES: Global Skills, Relationship Building, Sensitivity

RELATED BEHAVIORS, SKILLS, and ATTRIBUTES:

Global Skills	Recognize their organization's role in a multinational industry; see global opportunities and threats, are adept at doing business across borders and cultures.
Relationship Building	Recognize importance of relationships, devote energy to cultivating relationships, enjoy being around people, maintain broad internal and external networks of business relationships.
Sensitivity	Show empathy toward others; consider the feelings of others; value diversity.

OPERATING PRINCIPLE # 4: *Rely* **On Each Other**

COMPETENCIES: Relationship Building, Team Player, Team Management

RELATED BEHAVIORS, SKILLS, and ATTRIBUTES:

Relationship Building	Recognize importance of relationships; devote energy to cultivating relationships; enjoy being around people; maintain broad internal and external networks of business relationships.
Team Player	Share resources toward organizational goals; truly appreciate the synergy that teamwork can provide-the whole is often greater than the sum of the parts; actively communicate and build relationships with other team members.
Team Management	Identify team roles; set and communicate team goals; monitor team progress towards goals; actively work to maintain team focus; foster team atmosphere and reward collaboration.

OPERATING PRINCIPLE # 5: *Promote* **Both Individual and Team Values**

COMPETENCIES: Global Skills, Integrity, Relationship Building, Sensitivity

RELATED BEHAVIORS, SKILLS, and ATTRIBUTES:

Global Skills	Recognize their organization's role in a multinational industry; see global opportunities and threats, are adept at doing business across borders and cultures.
Integrity	Are honest with themselves and others; maintain ethical standards; foster an ethical environment; assume personal responsibility
Relationship Building	Recognize importance of relationships; devote energy to cultivating relationships; enjoy being around people; maintain broad internal and external networks of business relationships.
Sensitivity	Show empathy toward others; consider the feelings of others; value diversity.

OPERATING PRINCIPLE # 6: *Seek* **Skillful, Adaptable Players**

COMPETENCIES: Adaptability, Learning Agility, Organizing and
Planning, Technical Expertise

RELATED BEHAVIORS, SKILLS, and ATTRIBUTES:

Adaptability	Are flexible and open to new ideas; are quick to adapt to new situations.
Learning Agility	Rapidly assimilate and use new information; seek new knowledge; foster a learning environment.
Organizing & Planning	Plan and organize so that work is accomplished efficiently; prioritize multiple, competing tasks; maximize use of available time; make efficient use of organization's resources.
Technical Expertise	Exhibit functional knowledge, bring unique expertise, maintain current technical skills.

OPERATING PRINCIPLE # 7: *Charge* **The Team To Perform The Work**

COMPETENCIES: Customer Orientation, Results Orientation, Visioning

RELATED BEHAVIORS, SKILLS, and ATTRIBUTES:

Customer Orientation	Anticipate and meet customer needs; are guided by customer expectations; solicit customer feedback; monitor market trends.
Results Orientation	Value outcomes; demonstrate sense of urgency; show desire to accomplish, make things happen; convey a continual pressure to achieve results quickly; balance short and long-term goals.
Visioning	Create a preferred future; communicate it enthusiastically; attract others to their vision

OPERATING PRINCIPLE # 8: *Empower* **Players To Win**

COMPETENCIES: Problem Solving and Decision Making, Risk
Taking

RELATED BEHAVIORS, SKILLS, and ATTRIBUTES:

Problem Solving and Decision Making	Approach problems and decisions methodically; isolate causes from symptoms; withhold judgment while gathering information; involve others as appropriate; commit to action-act readily and decisively; demonstrate sound judgment.
Risk Taking	Try new things; find a balance between analysis and action; are able to fail and learn from it; are open to criticism

OPERATING PRINCIPLE # 9: *Coach* **Teams To Respond To Changing Conditions On Their Own**

COMPETENCIES: Mission Focus, Strategic Thinking

RELATED BEHAVIORS, SKILLS, and ATTRIBUTES:

Mission Focus	Understand the core purpose of the enterprise; incorporate mission into daily activities; communicate mission and interpret application for team; value the mission, believe in it, and stand behind it.
Strategic Thinking	Demonstrate an orientation to the future; develop and maintain long-term plans and constantly measure progress against them; communicate strategy to team members; make decisions and take actions within a strategic context.

OPERATING PRINCIPLE # 10: *Develop* **Partners On The Field**

COMPETENCIES: Active Communication, Coaching and Counseling, Delegation, Influence, Relationship Building

RELATED BEHAVIORS, SKILLS, and ATTRIBUTES:

Active Communication	Actively seek and share information; use modern technologies to facilitate timely communications; create an open and accessible environment that encourages flow of information; ensure that their employees have current and accurate information.
Coaching & Counseling	See themselves as coaches; set specific goals and communicate them clearly; monitor progress toward goals; offer clear, direct, and timely feedback; provide training, direction, and support to fit individual needs.
Delegation	Assign work to others; release authority within set boundaries; provide resources needed for success; monitor progress; empower subordinates.
Influence	Motivate, persuade, and excite others; adjust style to fit situation; have presence, confidence, style; maintain a personal power base (honest, fair, open).
Relationship Building	Recognize importance of relationships; devote energy to cultivating relationships; enjoy being around people; maintain broad internal and external networks of business relationships.

OPERATING PRINCIPLE # 11: *Achieve* **Cross-Cultural Agility**

COMPETENCIES: Global Skills, Learning Agility, Relationship
Building, Self Objectivity

RELATED BEHAVIORS, SKILLS, and ATTRIBUTES:

Global Skills	Recognize their organization's role in a multinational industry; see global opportunities and threats; are adept at doing business across borders and cultures
Learning Agility	Rapidly assimilate and use new information; seek new knowledge; foster a learning environment.
Relationship Building	Recognize importance of relationships; devote energy to cultivating relationships; enjoy being around people; maintain broad internal and external networks of business relationships.
Self Objectivity	Know their own strengths and limitations; are aware of their impact on others; value self-knowledge; are open to feedback and use it for self-improvement.

Acknowledgments

I would like to acknowledge and thank the following people. Their influence on my thinking over the years—and conceptual contributions—were invaluable in helping me prepare this book.

Peter McIntosh for writing his book *Physical Education In England Since 1800,* where he chronicles the history and influence of organized games to the education of its citizens in the 1800s.

William Bridges for pointing out in his book *Job Shift,* how the present nature of business is changing from a "job" structure to a "work" structure...and why football serves as an inadequate metaphor in business for the future.

Jon Katzenbach and Douglas Smith for describing the importance—and workings—of "real" teams in future business, in their seminal book, *The Wisdom of Teams.*

Richard Farson for reminding all of us in his book *Management of The Absurd,* that good managers transcend technique...

Jennifer James for introducing the argument in her book *Thinking In The Future Tense,* that understanding the nature of change is harder today because of the dated nature of the signs and signals to explain the future.

Warren Bennis for being one of the first to describe in his book *On Becoming A Leader,* how the new global model functions like an interdependent network...and what effective leadership looks like under that model.

Researchers at the Conference Board for their work identifying five areas that need to change if global teams are to work.

The GLOBE Program Researchers for their work in identifying 22 specific attributes and behaviors viewed universally across cultures as contributing to leadership effectiveness in their book *Culture, Leadership and Organizations: The GLOBE Study of 62 Societies.*

In writing *The Collaborator,* I recruited an army of collaborators. In the beginning, a number of old friends, a few relatives, and teammates at work were introduced to the book. Among them were Doug Brockbank, Loren Lee, Tom Hurd, Karen Jenkins, Ron Jenkins, Jeff McMillian, Barbara Pittman, Rob Moore, Gary Stone, and Jaime Vega. Later on I added more recruits: Karen Natzel, Sylvia Lindman, Jeanne Coyle, Abby Haight, Dan Terry, Gayle Buskuhl, Carl Giavanti, Dave Underhill, Tim Blakesly, Jim Sutton, and Richard Hodge. As the book progressed, I sought out other colleagues: Jon Anastasio, John Cochran, Bob Phillips, Bruce Griffiths, Dave Jennings, Rich Doherty, and John Hoskins. Throughout the writing of the book, I persisted in seeking ongoing feedback from Tom Hurd, Jeff McMillian, and Bruce Griffiths. Special thanks to these gentlemen for staying with me on the project. Near the book's completion, Nancy Hill was recruited as my professional editor for the manuscript. Her collaborative style made the task of completing the project a very enjoyable one. A big thanks also goes to Brian Mount and Marcia Hooper at YRG for recruiting Tina Swanson, who produced the book cover. Last, I wish to thank my wife, Dee Dee, for putting up with my "disappearing" act in the evenings to write this book.

About the Author

Winsor Jenkins currently serves as Vice President, Human Resources for Northwest Pipe Company, a NASDAQ traded international manufacturing firm in Vancouver, Washington. He has worked as a senior level, human resources professional in a variety of multinational businesses in the United States, Canada, and Mexico, including optics, pulp and paperboard, consumer products, forest products, and metals.

He received his B.S. from Cornell University and his M.B.A. from the University of Idaho.

He has written articles on leadership development for the *Soccer Journal*, the official publication of the National Soccer Coaches Association of America and *Human Resources Planning*, the journal of the Human Resources Planning Society.

Winsor has played, coached, and refereed soccer.

10560921R10076

Made in the USA
San Bernardino, CA
19 April 2014